The World in a Nutshell

Iraq
in a nutshell

*

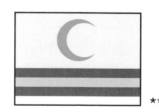

**

Enisen Publishing

Iraq in a Nutshell

* Saddam Hussein's Flag:
The flag of Iraq under Saddam Hussein's rule was adopted on July 31, 1963 and had three bands of red, white and black (top, center and bottom) with three green five-pointed stars. The words "Allahu akbar" (God is great) in Arabic script were added in January 1991 during the Gulf War to give the flag (and Hussein's regime) a more Islamic appearance.

** Proposed Future Flag:
In 2004, the American-led Iraqi Governing Council approved the design of a new flag with a white background (standing for peace) and two blue stripes (representing Iraq's Shi'ites and Sunnis and the Tigris and Euphrates rivers) flanking a yellow stripe meant to represent the Kurds (from the color of the star on the flag of Kurdistan). A blue crescent, symbolizing Islam, floats above the lines. The flag was initially met with criticism by the Iraqis because of its resemblance to the Israeli flag which has two light blue horizontal stripes on a white background with a Star of David in the center.
Saddam Hussein's flag will continue to be used until a permanent Iraqi government is installed.

***

Note: This book uses the initials B.C. ("before Christ") and A.D. ("Anno Domini" or "in the year of the Lord") rather than B.C.E. ("Before the Common Era") and C.E. (in the Common Era") to designate years since the writer and editors felt these terms were more familiar to Nutshell Notes readers.
We understand that future activities may modify or shed new light on some of the data in this book. For that reason, Nutshell Notes, LLC and Enisen Publishing invite readers to visit our website www.enisen.com to learn about the latest developments concerning Iraq.

Iraq in a Nutshell
First edition – March 2003
First published – March 2003
Second edition – September 2004

Enisen Publishing
2118 Wilshire Boulevard, #351
Santa Monica, CA 90403-5784
(866) ENISENP 866 364-7367
http://www.enisen.com
publishing@enisen.com

Text	Amanda Roraback
Maps	Katie Gerber
Editor	Paul Bernhard
Editor-in-Chief	Dorothy Roraback

Library of Congress Cataloging-in-Publication Data:
Library of Congress Control Number: 2004111750
ISBN 0-9702908-6-1
Printed in the United States of America

TABLE OF CONTENTS

Iraq in a Nutshell

FACTS AND FIGURES

Country Name: Republic of Iraq

Local Long Form: Al Jumhuriyah al Iraqiyah

Capital City: Baghdad

Independence: October 3, 1932 from League of Nations mandate under British administration

Population: 25,374,691 (July 2004 est.)

Ethnic Groups: Arab 75-80%, Kurdish 15-20%, Turkomen, Assyrian and others 5%

Religion: 97% Muslim (Shi'a 60-65%, Sunni 32-37%), Christian or other 3%

Languages: Arabic is the official language of Iraq, Kurdish is official in the Kurdish Autonomous Region, Assyrian, Armenian

Literacy: Total population 40.4%, male 55.9%, female 24.4% (2003 est.)

Currency: 1 Iraqi Dinar = 1000 fils or 20 dirhams.

Exports: Oil has traditionally provided about 95% of foreign exchange earnings.
War (Iran-Iraq War, Gulf War I and II) has interrupted Iraq's oil production and foreign sanctions (including the oil-for-food program begun in 1996) have forced Iraq to limit its trade of oil in exchange for food and medicines.

Export partners: US 37.4%, Taiwan 7.7%, Canada 7.5%, France 7.5%, Jordan 6.9%, Netherlands 5.8%, Italy 4.9%, Morocco 4.3%, Spain 4.1% (2002)

Proven Oil Reserves: 113.8 billion bbl (1 January 2002)

Currency: In January 2004, the new Iraqi dinar became Iraq's official currency. Pictures of an ancient Babylonian ruler, a 10th century mathematician and an Islamic compass replace images of Saddam Hussein on the new bills.

GDP per capita: $1600 per year

Size: 168,709 square miles, roughly the size of California (36 miles of coastline)

Major Cities: Baghdad, Basra, Mosul, Karbala, Kirkuk

Figures taken from the CIA World Factbook 2004 – Iraq

ANCIENT HISTORY

With all the violence surrounding Iraq today, it is hard to believe that the country's borders roughly correspond to the area considered the "cradle of civilization." The ancient region of Mesopotamia (which also included part of present-day Syria) developed from the Fertile Crescent between the Tigris and Euphrates Rivers, where some of the earliest agricultural communities flourished more than 10,000 years ago.

To support their settled lifestyle, these communities built irrigation systems, domesticated animals, used wheeled devices and developed sophisticated systems of writing, law, mathematics, religion and other concepts that became the bases of modern-day civilization.

SUMERIANS (2900 B.C.-2000 B.C.)

The Sumerians who moved to Mesopotamia (meaning "between the rivers" in Greek) 5000 years ago learned to tame the unpredictable rivers with complex irrigation systems and tilled the lands with the earliest known plows. As a result, the cultivators were able to grow surplus crops that could be transported to the villages via canals and innovative donkey-pulled wheeled carts. This freed the rest of the non-farming population to follow other pursuits.

To facilitate the distribution of the harvests and manage the property, the Sumerians also introduced the first form of writing. Commercial transactions were documented on stone tablets in **cuneiform** (a method of writing using wedge-shaped symbols) and by using mathematical formulae based on a "sexigesimal" system (based on numerical 60 as opposed to our base ten which is "decimal"). The modern-day 24-hour clock, which is divided into 60 minutes and 60 seconds, still derives directly from this system.

As great city-states developed around the settled population, new classes of bureaucrats and judges were employed to mediate transactions and keep order. It was at this time, moreover, that the code of law later made famous by Babylonian King **Hammurabi** in the 18th century B.C. took root.

Although the various city-states became more consolidated as the larger communities swallowed the smaller ones, the empire was not cohesive enough to withstand the invasion of another group of people, the **Akkadians**, who had migrated up from the Arabian Peninsula. However, the Sumerian culture was preserved.

AKKADIANS (2340 B.C. – 2125 B.C.)

The Akkadian kingdom, which was ruled form its capital city of Akkad (renamed Babylon by subsequent conquerors), absorbed most of the Sumerian culture and let the existing communities have nominal control of most of their defeated city-states. By adopting the Sumerian system of government, economy, law, religion and even their folklore, the Akkadians virtually became Sumerians themselves and spread the culture over their vast empire which reached as far as Lebanon.

AMORITES OR OLD BABYLONIANS (1900 B.C. – 1600 B.C.)

Like the Akkadians before them, the Amorites ruled from Akkad, which they renamed Babylon, giving them the name "Old Babylonians, " and adopted much of Sumerian culture and customs. Unlike the Sumerians, however, the Amorites consolidated the populace under the rule of a monarch whose power was believed to have divine origins. They developed a body of law based on the tenets of Amorite and Sumerian concepts, but doled out harsher punishments, most familiarly the taking of an "eye for an eye" and "a tooth for a tooth." The *lex talionis* or **Law of Retribution** , set in writing by Babylonian King **Hammurabi** in the 18th century B.C., is considered the earliest comprehensive legal code known in history.

HITTITES (1600 B.C. – 1100 B.C.)

The Hittites also adopted the ways of the communities that they vanquished in the 17th century B.C. and spread Mesopotamian customs and ideas throughout their empire to Syria, Palestine and eventually to Egypt and Greece and other cultures around the Mediterranean. Mass migrations that took place in the second millennium B.C. from Europe towards Persia and India and back (introducing the Kassites who ruled central Mesopotamia from 1500-1200 B.C.) further cultivated the spread of ideas throughout the region.

ASSYRIANS (1200 B.C. – 612 B.C.)

After the Kassite invasion, Babylon and the rest of Mesopotamia was conquered by militaristic Semitic peoples called Assyrians who set up their capital in the new city of **Nineveh**. The Assyrians had the largest standing army in the region at that time and used the most technologically innovative weapons to overtake communities from as far as Armenia and Mesopotamia to present-day Syria and Palestine/Israel. In order to prevent revolts in the occupied areas, they forced conquered peoples to migrate to other areas in the empire.

For example, after the Assyrians took **Samaria** or "The House of Israel" (the Hebrew's northern kingdom), they forced the conquered Israelites to relocate to Mesopotamia. In their new land, the relocated Hebrews assimilated into the existing society and became eternally known as the "Ten Lost Tribes" in Jewish history.

IRAQ IN THE BIBLE

* The **Garden of Eden** is believed to have been located in Iraq.

* The birthplace of Abraham was in **Ur**, in present-day Iraq.

* The story of **Noah** and the flood resembles a Sumerian legend about an old man who survived 40 days and 40 nights of rain in an ark - recounted in the **Epic of Gilgamesh**

* The actual **Tower of Babel** was built in Iraq to honor the Babylonian god Marduk.

The Assyrians were finally defeated in 612 B.C. by insurgents from the city-state of Babylon who burned Nineveh to the ground.

CHALDEANS OR NEW BABYLONIANS (612 B.C.-539 B.C.)

Under the greatest of the "New Babylonians," **King Nebuchadnezzar II** (605-562 B.C.), Babylon was restored to its former splendor. The most famous city in the world was adorned with a new temple (the **Tower of Babel**) built to honor the Babylonian god **Marduk**, and the legendary **Hanging Gardens of Babylon**, still considered one of the seven wonders of the ancient world though no longer in existence.

Like the Assyrians, the Chaldeans also adopted the practice of relocating conquered people to other areas. After **Nebuchadnezzar** occupied the southern Jewish kingdom of **Judea** (or Judah) in 587 B.C., he moved the remaining Hebrew population to Mesopotamia. Unlike the "lost tribes," though, the Judean Hebrews or "Jews" remained intact during their Babylonian captivity and continued to develop the Jewish religion. It was during their time in captivity, in fact, that the Jews began to pen the **Torah**, established synagogues and established the direction of prayer (towards the lost Temple in Jerusalem). Daily the Jews promised that they would one day return to Jerusalem to rebuild the Holy Temple that had been destroyed by Nebuchadnezzar. Even today, Jews punctuate prayers and greetings with the phrase "next year in Jerusalem." When the Babylonian Empire fell to the Persians a few decades later, the Hebrews had their wish and returned.

Vestiges of the Hebrew's Mesopotamian sojourn are still very evident in the pages of the Hebrew Scriptures.

PERSIAN EMPIRE (539 B.C. – 331 B.C.)

The Persians entered Mesopotamia in 539 B.C. from the region north of the Persian Gulf (modern-day Iran). Motivated by **Cyrus the Great**, the Persians believed that it was their religious duty to propagate the ideals of **Zoroastrianism** (the religious system of the ancient Persians that teaches the eventual triumph of good over evil) by dominating the world.

By the time Cyrus's grandson, **Darius I**, took power in 522 B.C., the Persian Empire extended from India to Macedon (northeast of Greece). The Persian expansion, though, was halted in 490 B.C. by the Greek Athenians in the momentous **Battle of Marathon** and the Persians were finally conquered a century and a half later by the armies of **Alexander the Great**.

SELEUCID EMPIRE (323 B.C. – 170 B.C.)

After Alexander's death in Babylon in 323 B.C., his empire was divided among three generals. **Ptolemy** was given control of Egypt, **Antigone** ruled Greece and Alexander's military commander **Seleucus** governed Mesopotamia, Syria and Persia.

PARTHIANS (A.D. 170- A.D. 224), SASSANIANS (A.D. 224-A.D. 637)

The Seleucid Empire fell to the Parthians who invaded in 170 B.C. from what is today Iran, and in AD 224 were themselves conquered by the Sassanians (also from Iran) forever ending Greek control over Mesopotamia.

INTRODUCTION OF ISLAM

The course of history was drastically changed when a man, born in A.D. 570 in Mecca (in modern-day Saudi Arabia), was acknowledged as the last prophet of God (or "**Allah**" to the Muslims). The prophet, **Mohammed**, united the formally polytheistic tribes of Arabia under the monotheistic (believing in one god) banner of Islam and spread Allah's messages, chronicled in the **Quran**, throughout the region. After his death in 632, his followers spread the religion of Islam throughout Arabia under Mohammed's successor (or *caliph*), **Abu Bakr** (632-634) and later over Palestine, Syria, and Egypt under the leadership of the second caliph, **Umar ibn al Khattab** (634-644).

The new religion first reached Mesopotamia in A.D. 634 when an army of Arab Muslims under the leadership of **General Khalid ibn al Walid**. Nicknamed the "Sword of Islam," Walid fought the vastly technically and numerically superior Persian **Sassanids** in the "**Battle of the Chains**" — so-named because the Persian troops purportedly were chained together to prevent them from fleeing.

During another victorious battle in A.D. 636, the badly outnumbered Arabs again routed the Persian Sassanids, forcing the vanquished troops to embrace Islam or pay a tribute tax (*jizya*) to the Muslims. The memory of this "**Battle of Qasiya** (or **Qadisiyah**)" was revived centuries later by **Saddam Hussein** when he claimed his own numerically inferior Iraqi Arab troops could again defeat the larger army of Persians fighting the Iran-Iraq war.

The ultimate collapse of the Sassanid Empire in A.D. 638 marked the beginning of Arabic dominance in the region, the establishment of Islam as the official religion and the dawn of the golden age of Muslim culture.

In 762, **Abd al Abbas**, the 1st Caliph (divine-right ruler of Muslims) of the **Abbasid Dynasty**, founded the city of **Baghdad** near ancient Babylon and made it the political seat of the Caliphate and the capital of the Islamic world. By the 10th century, the city had become the intellectual center of the world, second in size only to Constantinople, and hosting philosophers, scholars, scientists, and a bevy of traders traveling along the Silk Route which connected Asia with the Mediterranean.

At the height of its splendor, Baghdad had a university, many palaces and a teaching hospital and produced some of the greatest minds of the time. **Muhammad ibn Musa al-Khawarizmi** (680-750), for example, is credited with the invention of Algebra and the application of the Hindu numeric system (today called Arabic numerals) to modern mathematics.

Baghdad's glory began to fade near the end of the 10th century when the center of Muslim intellectual life shifted from Baghdad to the seat of the **Fatimid dynasty** in the newly developed city of Cairo, Egypt. The competition between Baghdad and Cairo continued from that point on.

The Abbasid Caliphate had weakened under the strain of the religious schism between the **Shi'ites** and **Sunni Muslims** (see chapter on Shi'ites p. 37) and finally succumbed to the Shi'ite Persian Buwayhids in 945 and Sunni Turkish Seljuks in 1045.

The Shi'ite Fatimids were held at bay by the military might of the Sunni Seljuks, whose empire included Iran, Iraq and Syria as were the Byzantines whose defeat in 1071 at the Battle of Manzikert, opened the way for Turkish occupation of Anatolia. But the Seljuks were not able to counter the increasing power of the Mongols from Central Asia.

MONGOLS

Passing through from China to Europe in 1258, the Mongol horde, led by **Hulagu Khan** (1217-1265) the grandson of the infamous Ghengis Khan, stopped in Baghdad long enough to massacre its citizens, destroy the Caliphate, plunder the country's riches, wreck the irrigation canals, leave the countryside in ruin and flatten cities they passed through. Although the Mongols didn't hold the region for very long, they caused enough damage to obliterate Baghdad's splendor for centuries.

TAMERLANE

The Mesopotamian region was subjected to another brutal conquest in 1401 by the Turkish regent, **Timur the Lame** or **Tamerlane** (1336-1405). Tamerlane entered Mesopotamia from Samarkand dealing a final blow to the already weakened nation.

By the time of Tamerlane's conquest, Iraq had been suffering a severe economic depression due to the destruction of its farming capabilities and the loss of its status as a commercial center. The urban way of life in Iraq had also given way to the revival of a tribal-based system of regional rulers (a system that continued until modern times[1]) making the country even more vulnerable to attack.

As Tamerlane's empire disintegrated in the 16th century the region was powerless against its powerful neighbors, the Turkish Sunni Ottomans and the Shi'ite Persians. For the next four centuries the area became a battleground for these competing empires as well as the frontline for the continuing conflict between Sunni and Shi'ite Muslims.

SAFAVID PERSIANS (Shi'ite) (1501-1683)

The Safavids grew from a Turkish **Sufi** order as a puritanical reaction to the

---

[1] Saddam Hussein regularly selected members of his Tikriti tribe to fill governmental and military posts.

adulteration of Islam by the Mongol infidels. When **Ismail I** (1501-1524), the King of Tabriz (northeastern Iran), assumed control of the Safavids in the 16th century, he proclaimed Shi'ism the new state religion and, as Shah of Iran, forced the religion on the rest of his kingdom. To this day, Iran is almost entirely Shi'ite.

As Shi'as, the Safavids were particularly interested in securing control of what is now Iraq because it was the home of the Shiite's two holiest cities, **Najaf** and **Karbala.** They also hoped to incorporate the Shi'as living in southern Mesopotamia into their own empire.

But their entitlement was challenged by the Sunni Ottoman sultans, who refuted the Shah's assertion that he was the rightful head of the entire Muslim community. The Ottomans sought control of Iraq as a Sunni bulwark against the spread of Shi'ism to the rest of the region. They hoped to retain Baghdad, the old capital of the Abbasid Empire, which had its own symbolic significance to the Sunni Turks of the Ottoman Empire.

OTTOMAN TURKS (Sunni) 1301-1918)
Founded around 1300 by **Sultan Osman I**, the Ottoman state was just one of many Turkish states that emerged in the wake of the collapsing Seljuk Turk Empire. By absorbing the other leftover Turkish dynasties, the Ottomans built the foundation for an Islamic empire that eventually stretched from southeastern Europe across the Middle East to the borders of Persia. The Ottomans ruled their great empire from their capital in Istanbul (former Byzantine Constantinople) for the next 400 years, although much of that time was spent fighting to maintain the realm.

In order to manage the vast Ottoman territory while the leaders were occupied fighting against the Europeans and Persians, the Ottomans divided the region into *vilayets*, or "administrative districts." The area that became the forerunner of "Iraq," for example, was comprised of three *vilayets*: Mosul in the north, where most of the Kurds lived, Baghdad in the middle, and the primarily Shi'ite *vilayet* of Basra in the south.[2]

From the 16th to the 17th centuries, control over modern-day Iraq shifted back and forth between the Persian Safavids and the Turkish Ottomans (with brief stints under the Mamelukes), with none of the victors undertaking measures to develop the area. Despite some efforts by reform-minded governor **Midhat Pashta** in 1869, and some Sultans before him, to repair and modernize the *vilayets* of Basra, Baghdad and Mosul, the cities of Mesopotamia languished, leaving Iraq the most backward and underdeveloped region in the Ottoman Empire.

---

[2] Saddam Hussein and other Iraqis later claimed that Kuwait, whose borders were within the Ottoman vilayet of Basra when the empire collapsed, was technically part of Iraq. The Kuwaitis countered that the country's independence from the Ottoman Empire long preceded that of Iraq's (see Gulf War).

EUROPEAN INTERFERENCE

In 1908, a new ruling clique, the **Young Turks**, who took power in Istanbul, endeavored to unity the Ottoman Empire along secular lines and govern according to Western models. This nationalist group also tried to homogenize the empire by imposing Turkish customs, language and policies on the diverse Ottoman society. The **"turkification"** movement, which alienated much of the empire's non-Turkish members, including the Arab Iraqis, eventually sparked revolts throughout the empire, precipitating the empire's decline.

Backed and encouraged by the British and inspired by other nationalist uprisings taking place in the world at that time, the Iraqis revolted against their Turkish overlords in 1917. But the loosely integrated tribes of the Basra, Baghdad and Mosul *vilayets* were powerless to protect their newly independent nation against the ambitions of the more powerful European countries.

Britain and France were both interested in gathering up the spoils that would be left behind after the great Ottoman Empire collapsed. Britain hoped to acquire a new route to its prized imperialist territory, India, and the Germans hoped to use the land to build a railroad from Berlin through Baghdad to the Persian Gulf.

Of even greater strategic importance was the desire to have access to the oil that was discovered in that part of the world (see <u>Politics of Oil</u>, p.51) For the British, who had no oil of their own, the decision by Lord of the Admiralty (and future Prime Minister) **Winston Churchill** to power the country's naval ships by burning oil instead of coal made the commodity particularly vital. With the outbreak of the **First World War** and the Ottoman Empire's decision to ally itself with the Germans, moreover, the British were extremely anxious about competitive interest in the region.

WWI

To hedge their bets and ensure the collapse of the Ottoman Empire, the British backed already fomenting rebellions against the Ottomans by the Arab populace. Acting as a British liaison officer, **T.E. Lawrence** (popularly known as **Lawrence of Arabia**), became famous for his role in organizing Arab tribal fighters, inspired by European promises of independence after the Ottoman Empire's demise, into an effective force against the Ottoman Turks.

Soon after the British captured Baghdad in 1917, the Ottoman Empire collapsed and the British were in control of the three Ottoman *vilayets* (Mosul, Baghdad and Basra) that would eventually become Iraq.

BRITISH MANDATE

While the Arabs rejoiced in their imminent autonomy, the British were working out the details of the **Sykes-Picot Agreement** of 1916 which, rather than granting independence to the Arabs, divvied up the territories of the former Ottoman Empire between the victorious European nations. Under the agreement, France would assume temporary administrative control (or **"mandate"**) over Syria and Lebanon, and Britain would have a mandate over Palestine (including Transjordan), the Gulf States (including Kuwait) and Iraq.

The Arabs living in Mesopotamia, however, were not keen on the prospect of one imperial power replacing another and, putting aside their ethnic, religious and cultural differences, openly expressed their discontent.

The ensuing insurrection began in 1919 with the murder of a British officer and reached its zenith in 1920 when the mandate was finalized at the **San Remo Conference**. The severity and cost of putting down the rebels led the British to reconsider the mandate and sponsor a more legitimate candidate to head the state of Iraq. **King Faisal** -- a Hashemite ruler (or *sharif*) from Saudi Arabia who claimed to be a direct descendent of the Prophet Mohammed -- appeared to fit the bill.

Along with his Islamic credentials, Faisal had also fought alongside T.E. Lawrence against the Ottomans during WWI and was sympathetic to the British. The fact that Faisal was a Saudi (and Sunni) rather than an Iraqi, Shi'ite, strained his relationship with natives. At the same time, the differences guaranteed that he would never feel secure enough to alienate himself by challenging the British.

The British also figured that a Sunni-led regime (despite the fact that the country had a Shi'ite majority) would be more acceptable to Iraq's primarily Sunni neighbors. They believed that the Sunnis, furthermore, would be more inclined to favor modernization than the reactionary Shi'a clerics and their followers. The Sunnis ran the government of Iraq from that point on.

In order to strengthen King Faisal's questionable legitimacy as an Iraqi leader, a carefully calculated plebiscite (election), held by the British in 1921 after all viable competition was eliminated, demonstrated a 96% endorsement by the Iraqis. With superficial political approval, the puppet Hashemite king ruled the country under British authority until agitation by Iraqi nationalists, tribal leaders and even the King himself brought about a series of measures granting the regime greater and greater autonomy. In 1932, after years of lobbying, the British mandate finally came to an end and the country of Iraq was admitted into the **League of Nations** as an independent nation.

9

Faisal died a year later and was succeeded by his son **Ghazi.** Despite Iraq's continued economic dependence on Great Britain, Ghazi cast his allegiance in a different direction from his father. In 1936, Ghazi signed a nonaggression treaty with Saudi Arabia and formed an alliance with other Arab nations. His pan-Arab interests and anti-British sentiments, which made him popular with many Iraqis, were believed to be the cause of his mysterious death in 1939.

In 1939, Ghazi's son and successor, **Faisal II,** was only 3 years old when his father died. Until he came of age, the new monarchy was governed by a regent, **Amir abd al Ilah,** and an Iraqi politician **Nuri as-Said,** both staunchly pro-British.

Said and Ilah's pro-western stance was increasingly at odds with the rest of the Arab world, especially after events such as Egyptian president **Gamal Abdel Nasser's** successful nationalization of the **Suez Canal** in Egypt (1956) and in light of growing bitterness over the high-handed treatment of the Palestinians by the British in Israel.

After almost three decades of British-backed Saudi rule in Iraq, the monarchy was finally toppled and the country experienced its first taste of republican government.

COUP D'ETAT

Because the regime under Said and Ilah (and by 1958, the now-grown Faisal II), didn't tolerate political dissent, opposition groups were forced to operate underground. It was one of these groups (called the **"Free Officers"**) led by Brigadier **Abdel Karim Kassim,** that staged the decisive coup d'etat against the monarchy in 1958, by killing the entire royal family, including the king's uncle and regent Ilah, the prime minister **Nuri Said** (who was caught trying to escape by dressing as a woman) and supporters.

Five years later, (1963) Kassim's government, itself, was toppled by a coup that, some say, was supported by the American CIA who regarded the shift as a "pro-Western re-orientation in the Middle East."

BAATH PARTY

The **Baath** (meaning "resurgence" or "rebirth" in Arabic) began as a secular political movement in Syria in the 1930s with the intention of reawakening the common culture of the Arab world in opposition to western influences imposed by the imperialistic British and French. It was formally founded in 1947 as the Arab Baath Socialist Party and achieved political power in Syria soon after. By 1963, the Baath Party was the only party in Syria and, in fulfillment of its socialist agenda, nationalized the country.

The Syrian-based Baath party, which had chapters all over the Arab world, campaigned for the equitable distribution of oil wealth (which was concentrated in the hands of a few, mostly foreign capitalists) and state ownership

of natural resources. It also called for the destruction of the artificial boundaries created by the British and French from the carved-up remains of the
Ottoman Empire hoping to eventually incorporate all the Arab chapters of
the party under a single leader.

The Iraqi chapter of the Baath party was founded in 1952 by **Fuad ar
Ribaki,** under the same banner of Unity, Freedom and Socialism as its
Syrian parent. Unlike the Syrian branch, though, the Iraqi Baathists
remained a small fringe group of intellectuals for most of the 1950s.

The Baathists first asserted their authority in 1959 by attempting to assassi-
nate President **Abdel Karim Kassim** (who had taken over the government
after the coup against the British-backed monarchy) because of his per-
ceived close relationship to the Baath's enemies, the Soviet-backed commu-
nists. Official biographers of Iraq's future president, Saddam Hussein, celebrated Hussein's role in the attempted coup. Other historians, however,
such as Con Coughlin, who wrote, Saddam: King of Terror,claim that
Hussein himself was partly responsible for the coup's failure by premature-
ly opening fire.

In 1963, the Baathists finally succeeded in removing and killing Kassim, but
could not muster up enough political muscle to hold onto power. In their
place, a larger and more moderate group led by General **Abdul Salam Arif**
took control.

Yet within five years, the Baathists had recruited enough new members and
supporters to stage a final and decisive coup against Arif's son **(Salam Arif**
who died in a helicopter accident in 1966). **Ahmed Hassan al-Bakr** was
installed as the new leader and the date, July 17, 1968, was declared the day
of "The Great Revolution that ended Iraq's dictatorial regime." To help
guarantee the new regime's survival, the Baathists immediately purged the
country of all dissidents.

SADDAM HUSSEIN

Saddam Hussein was born in April, 1937 (according to official records) in a tribal village near the city of **Tikrit** in north-central Iraq. His household, like those of other impoverished families living in the village, had no running water and no electricity. The family was so poor, in fact, that Hussein was often sent to steal chickens and eggs to keep the family fed.

Saddam's father either died soon after Saddam was born (the official story) or deserted his mother – a scandalous affair in Iraq – leaving Saddam fatherless and the fodder for teasing and bullying by the other children. He was raised, instead, by an abusive stepfather whose family had an even lower social status in the village than his mother and biological father.

Most children in rural Iraq are born into a hierarchy of families, clans and tribes that command great allegiance and loyalty. Hussein, who came from the **al-Khattab** clan in the al-Bu Nasir tribe dominant in the Tikrit region, surrounded himself with family members and other Tikritis as he rose to power, believing that Tikriti tribe members would be more loyal than administrators from rival groups.

At age 10, Hussein was sent to Baghdad to live with his uncle **Adnan Khairallah Tulfah,** a devout Sunni Muslim with xenophobic views, particularly against the British and their puppet-monarchy ruling Iraq at the time. Khairallah, an avid Nazi-sympathizer who once wrote a pamphlet titled "Three Whom God should not have created: Persians, Jews and Flies," was a hero and mentor to Saddam. Saddam in turn, was Khairallah's protégée and, due to his uncle's clout, was proudly introduced to members of the Sunni elite who were just beginning to play leading roles in Iraqi politics. It was during his stay with his uncle, moreover, that the erstwhile illiterate Hussein first received an education -- although his grades weren't good enough for entrance into Baghdad's prestigious Military Academy (an omission that later fueled his military ambitions).

In keeping with the rural Iraqi custom of maintaining the bonds of kinship and tribal loyalty through intermarriage, Saddam eventually married his favorite uncle's daughter (and his first cousin), **Sajida Khari,** with whom he had two sons (**Uday** and **Qusay**), and three daughters.

Hussein began working for the Baath Party in 1956 in part as the party's hitman. In October, 1959, he participated in the faction's first attempted assassination of **General Kassim,** the prime minister installed in Iraq after the fall of the Hashemite royal family. Some sources claim that it was Hussein's blunders during the plot that caused it to fail. State biographers, however, lauded Hussein for his heroic role in the incident.

After the botched assassination attempt, Hussein and his fellow plotters escaped to Syria and Egypt where Hussein lived at the time of the Baath Party's second successful (but short-lived) coup against Kassim in 1963.

When the Baathists regained power permanently five years later, supreme authority was passed to **Bakr**, the chairman of the **Revolutionary Command Council,** (the executive and legislative arm of the Baath Party) who then became president and commander-in-chief of the armed forces. Saddam Hussein became the deputy chairman of the RCC in charge of internal security, a position he used to his great advantage.

For the next few years, Hussein ran the country from the sidelines using his position in Internal Security to rid the country of potential rivals to the Baath party (which was a minority movement at its inception) and, more significantly, his own enemies.

Always careful not to overstep his boundaries, Hussein dutifully carried out the orders of his uncle's friend and fellow Tikriti, President Bakr, while manipulating the system. As second in command, (Vice-President in 1973) Hussein was responsible for some of Iraq's most important developments. He orchestrated the nationalization of oil, for instance, by brokering an agreement with the Soviets pouring money into the country's coffers.

Oil revenues enabled the government to build schools, bring electricity to remote regions (like Saddam's home town), develop radio and TV networks (used to broadcast Baathist propaganda), build railroads, develop technology and participate in all types of modernizing endeavors.

To ensure that the entire country knew who was responsible for the changes, moreover, poor families around the country were given TV sets and Hussein's image appeared regularly in the news. (As president, Hussein reinforced the "cult of personality" by hiring doubles to appear for the media at various functions freeing the real Saddam Hussein to perform state tasks. The ruse also made it appear as if Saddam was omnipresent).

Due to his privileged relationship with President Bakr, Hussein was also able to install his friends, family members and clan associates in the highest governmental positions further reinforcing his authority.By the time Hussein was ready to take his place at the head of Iraq's government, therefore, he already had so much influence in the government that Bakr was simply asked to step down. In a smooth transition on July 17th, 1979 (the anniversary of the 1968 revolution) Bakr "retired" from public life and "voluntarily" handed the reins to Hussein. Three years later, Bakr was quietly killed after it was rumored that he was staging a comeback.

One of Hussein's first moves as President was to rid the government of any rivals still surviving after purges conducted in the 1970s. In a filmed spectacle a few days after assuming power, Hussein accused and put to death dozens of Baath Party members on charges of conspiracy -- initiating a gruesome system of obedience through intimidation, torture and the threat of death. Hussein, his family members and loyal cronies controlled the media, the army, police and security services. Trade unions and rival parties were banned and opposition was punishable by death.

IRAN-IRAQ WAR

While Saddam Hussein was climbing to the head of Iraq's government, the fundamental Shi'ite cleric, **Ayatollah Khomeini,** was leading his country, Iran, in an Islamic Revolution in 1979.

Khomeini's rise to power was threatening to Iraq in a number of ways. First, the Ayatollah who had been living in exile in Iraq since 1964, had recently been kicked out (in 1978). Second, Hussein feared that he Shi'ites living in Iraq (60% of the population) would be swept up in Iran's Shi'ite revolution and overthrow the mainly Sunni regime -- in fact, the Ayatollah did call on Iraq's Shi'ites to revolt against the Sunni Baathist regime and in response, Saddam exiled thousands of Iraqi Shi'ites to Iran. Third, the growing religious fervor in Iran threatened to ignite religious sentiments in secular Iraq. Fourth, Iraq feared that Khomeini would support Kurdish rebellions in northern Iraq as Iran had done in the past.

In the meantime, Iran's strength had been weakened by a purge of military leaders loyal to the **Shah** (Iran's former leader) and the instability of the revolution itself. The chaos gave Hussein the perfect opportunity to champion the cause of Sunni Islam for the rest of the Sunni Arab world and to win glory as a war hero at home. The battle could also be considered another chapter in the historical Persian versus Arab, Shi'ite versus Sunni rivalry that began in the 16th century.

The Iraqi regime hoped that by capturing **Kuzhistan,** a primarily Arab (not Persian) swath of land in western Iran, the country could get its hands on the area's rich oil reserves and possibly trigger an Arab revolution against the new Iranian Islamic government. (It didn't happen).

Officially, Iraq said it declared war on Iran in order to recapture the valuable **Shatt-al-Arab** waterway, Iraq's main shipping route to the Persian Gulf (see map p. 2). According to the **Algiers Agreement** of 1975, the international border between Iran and Iraq was placed at the center of the canal. Iraq had agreed on this in order to persuade Iran to withdraw support for the Kurds, who were threatening the stability of the Baath party in the north. In 1979, however, the Iraqi regime claimed that the arrangement was only temporary and that Iraq, in fact, had the right to control the entire waterway.

Troops were deployed soon after the Algiers Treaty was unilaterally cancelled by Hussein in September 1980, with confidence that despite Iran's vast size (three times the size of Iraq) the Iraqi military would quickly defeat the Persians (Iranians) – who were struggling in the midst of political turmoil and only had worn-out weapons with which to defend themselves.

But neither Hussein nor the country's military were prepared to counter such strong Iranian resolve. Persian clerics roused hundreds of thousands of religious zealots (including many children) to fight a holy war (*jihad*) against the infidel aggressors. This poorly trained, unarmed "**Army of 20 Million**" cleared minefields for the safe passage of tanks and rushed the Iraqi troops en masse with visions of martyrdom (dying for the cause of Islam) and glory. The Iraqi troops, in contrast, did not have the same spiritual resolve to vanquish their enemy. In fact, many Iraqi fighters were Shi'ite Muslims themselves who were reluctant to fight their religious brothers.

In Iran, jailed pilots and military forces were released from prison to join the war and military leaders began to take the place of religious clerics in leading the Persian troops to victory at all costs. The Iraqi generals, on the other hand, were committed to preventing casualties and were hindered by Hussein's insistence that all military personnel answer directly to him.

After an eight-year war of attrition, with neither side claiming any lasting victories, the war took on a global aspect. Western powers began to take notice during one of the "**Tanker Wars**" – battles in the Persian Gulf targeting oil tankers (and hence threatening oil prices) from around the world.

Although most western powers claimed neutrality in the Iran-Iraq War, the majority stood behind the "lesser of two evils" -- Iraq. By the war's end,[3] Iraq's political Sunni dominance and secular leanings were more appealing to its primarily Sunni Arab neighbors and the West. Still reeling over the Iranian American hostage crisis of 1979, moreover, the United States hoped to contain the fundamental Islamic Revolution brewing in Iran.

Although Iraq's desperate use of chemical weapons against Iran (in violation of the 1925 **Geneva Protocol** on the use of such weapons) would temporarily cause the West to reconsider its allegiances, in 1986 Saddam's nation received enough arms and ammunition to force Iran to negotiate. With the acceptance of **UN Security Resolution 598**, both sides returned to their prewar boundaries. The war was over, albeit with no territorial gains, a million people dead or wounded and the economic structure of both countries in ruins.

---

[3] In 1985, the US armed Iran to help counter earlier Iraq successes. The arms shipments later became known as the Iran-Contra Affair.

GULF WAR

Although Iraq's million-strong army was the largest and most powerful in the Arab world by the end of the 8-year war with Iran, the rest of the country was in shambles. Oil production had precipitously dropped during the Iran-Iraq war and many of the country's oil wells were damaged. Reconstruction costs were astronomical. War debts had reached $80 billion and there were no jobs for veterans returning from battle. And although Saddam tried to claim an Iraqi victory after the costly conflict, the nation was aware that his regime was responsible for a war that cost the nation hundreds of thousands of casualties with little to show for it. To make matters worse, the profits from oil (Iraq's primary export) had gone way down in the international market due to flooding by other oil producing countries (primarily Russia).

In an attempt to ease all of the country's problems in one fell swoop, Hussein turned his attention to **Kuwait**, a country that was a fraction of the size of Iraq's former foe, Iran, in terms of population and geographic size, with an enviable coastline and rich oil reserves.

By targeting Kuwait and forcing it to forgive Iraq's debt of $13 billion, Iraq hoped to intimidate other lender nations into following suit. Hussein also hoped that by attacking the oil-rich nation and curbing its oil producing capabilities, world oil prices would rise and eventually, Iraq could take hold of Kuwait's portion of the lucrative **Rumaila Oil Fields** for itself. (Iraq and Kuwait shared ownership of Rumaila, one of the largest proven oil deposits in the world).

IRAQ'S HISTORICAL CLAIM ON KUWAIT
Since the time of the country's creation after World War I from remnants of the Ottoman Empire, Iraqis have claimed Kuwait as their own. As part of the Basra *vilayet*, (one of three administrative areas that made up Iraq after the collapse of the Ottoman Empire), Iraqis believed Kuwait was intended to be included within Iraqi borders. The Kuwaiti issue had been popular in Iraq since British Mandate days and Saddam hoped that by invoking the historical claim, he could repair his political image. The Kuwaitis maintained that they were independent from the Ottomans long before Iraq's creation.

CONSENT IN THE WEST
Saddam expected that the international community, which had supported him against Khomeini's fundamental Shi'ite Muslims, would be sympathetic to Iraq's plight and turn a blind eye to his aggression against the small Gulf state.

In Hussein's mind, the United States (the most formidable superpower left after the fall of the Soviet Empire) had tacitly consented to the attack of Kuwait through US Ambassador to Iraq, **April Glaspie.** In a meeting between the Ambassador and Hussein on July 25, 1990, Glaspie assured

Saddam that the U.S. wanted to improve relations with Iraq and had "no opinion on Arab-Arab conflicts such as [Iraq's] dispute with Kuwait."

A few days later, Iraq declared war on Kuwait (which it labeled Iraq's **19th district**) on the grounds that Kuwait was deliberately driving down the price of oil by producing too much -- an act that Hussein said amounted to "economic warfare" against Iraq -- and illegally pumping oil from Iraq's half of the Rumaila oil field. Iraq also claimed that its forces had been "invited" to Kuwait by a rebellious faction that wanted Iraq's help in toppling Kuwait's monarchy.

ATTACK ON KUWAIT

After eight years of bloodshed ostensibly fought over access to the **Shatt-al-Arab** waterway, Hussein gave up full control of **Shatt-al-Arab** to its former enemy, Iran, in exchange for a guarantee that the Persians would not incite a Kurdish rebellion in the north while Iraq pursued Kuwait in the south.

Only seven hours after Iraq invaded Kuwait on August 2, 1990, the country was completely in Iraqi hands. The Kuwaitis were terrorized and the only member of Kuwait's royal family who remained in the country (the others had fled before the invasion) was shot.

Despite Hussein's belief that the rest of the world would sit idly by as his military marched into Kuwait, the invasion caused an international uproar. Not only was the attack unprovoked, but Saddam's new position close to the border of Saudi Arabia, (the world's largest oil producer) was an ominous threat to all oil-consuming nations.

Almost immediately after Iraqi troops had entered Kuwaiti soil, American President **George H. Bush** imposed an economic embargo on the country and, backed by an international coalition of 38 nations (including many Arab countries[4]), demanded that Iraq leave Kuwait immediately and unconditionally (**UN Resolution 678**). In preparation for Bush's campaign, dubbed **Operation Desert Shield,** the American president stationed 230,000 U.S. and allied troops in neighboring Saudi Arabia[5] under the command of **General Schwarzkopf.**

When the deadline for Hussein's withdrawal came and passed without any action, the allies made their move. The United State's military began conducting massive air strikes against Iraq during its **Desert Storm** offensive in January 1991, followed by a ground assault.

In an attempt to turn the allied attack into an Arab-Israeli (or East-West) conflict, Hussein tried to provoke Israel into joining the fight by firing **Scud**

---

[4] Arab participants included Egypt, Syria, Saudi Arabia, Kuwait and Turkey. Jordan and Iran did not join the coalition.

[5] The presence of non-Muslim troops stationed in Saudi Arabia (the home of Mecca and Medina, Islam's holiest cities) was greatly opposed by devout Sunni Muslims in the Arab world, despite the fact that Saudi Arabia had asked for America's help against Saddam Hussein.

Missiles at the country. Israeli involvement, he hoped, would turn the Arab countries (whose participation was vital for allied success) to his side. But in deference to the U.S.-led alliance, the Israelis held back retaliatory fire.

In the course of the battle, coalition forces destroyed roads, factories, electrical plants, oil refineries, transportation networks, government buildings, communications facilities, bridges and sewers leaving Iraq dependent on foreign expertise to rebuild the country. Unable to withstand the massive assault on its infrastructure, Iraq agreed to a UN cease-fire in February, 1991, all the conditions that went along with it.

SPARING SADDAM HUSSEIN
The United States had met its objectives: the unconditional withdrawal of Iraqi troops from Kuwait; the restoration of the Kuwaiti government; and stability in the Gulf. The overthrow of Saddam, although a desirable outcome for many participants, was not the aim of the coalition attack -- in part because of the involvement of Arab countries (who would have objected) and in compliance with former U.S. President **Gerald Ford's** 1976 **Executive Order #12333,** making it illegal for the U.S. to take part in assassination plots. In any case, the Americans expected Hussein's regime to collapse on its own within months under the pressure of the war and subsequent economic sanctions.

FOMENTING LOCAL UNREST
To hasten the process, the United States aired radio broadcasts in the country encouraging Iraqis to rise up against their defeated leader. Heeding the call, **Kurds** in the north and **Shi'ites Muslims** in southern Iraq did rebel against the dictator fully expecting the West to support their uprising. But the West did not come to their aid.

Although the U.S. hoped that the lost unrest would accelerate the collapse of Saddam's regime, America was not prepared to commit the resources needed to maintain peace in Iraq after the dissolution of the central government. Nor was it prepared to install a new Iraqi government or prevent attacks from neighboring countries hoping to take advantage of Iraq's weakness. Despite their encouragement, the allies decided that it was more important to curtail Iraq's ability to produce weapons of mass destruction.

RESOLUTION 687
According to the terms of **United Nations Resolution 687,** Iraq was ordered to acknowledge Kuwait's sovereignty, repatriate all Kuwaitis and compensate organizations involved in repairing the country and treating casualties. Most importantly Iraq was ordered to destroy all of its ballistic missile systems (**SCUDS**) with a range of more than 150 kilometers (about the distance between Iraq and Israel). To ensure that the Iraqis met their obligations, UN-managed weapons inspectors were deployed to monitor the disarmament process.

Faced with rebellions in the north and the south, Hussein had no choice but to agree to the United Nation's terms for a permanent cease-fire.

Once the UN was satisfied, though, Hussein set upon the Kurdish and Shi'ite insurrectionists with such a vengeance that the United Nations was forced to set up **"no-fly zones"** prohibiting Iraqi planes from flying north of the 36 latitude (where the Kurds were at risk of chemical weapon attacks from the air) and below the 32 latitude (to protect the Shi'ites).

WAR CASUALTIES

During the course of six weeks of fighting, the Iraqis had lost about 100,000 soldiers and tens of thousands of civilians, including hundreds of Iraqis killed during an allied attack on a bomb shelter believed to be housing weapons. Another 200,000 Iraqi soldiers surrendered.

Although the allies reported only 150 casualties during the fighting, some sources claimed that more than 100,000 American service members sent to the region during the war continued to suffer from the so-called **"Gulf War Syndrome,"** a collection of maladies including fatigue, muscle pain, memory loss, sleep disorders with no determinant cause.

SANCTIONS

Immediately following Hussein's annexation of Kuwait in August, 1990, the UN imposed economic sanctions on Iraq. The sanctions continued after the conclusion of the war to pressure Iraq into complying with the demands of **UN Resolution 687** and to limit Saddam's ability to rebuild his army and fund his weapons program.

The maintenance of the economic embargo became controversial after reports revealed that thousands of Iraqis (mostly children) were dying every month because of deteriorating health conditions and shortages of food and clean water. A **"food-for-oil"** provision was enacted in 1995 (**Resolution 986**) to ease the suffering by allowing Iraq to sell limited amounts of oil under strict UN supervision in exchange for humanitarian goods, but the Iraqi population continued to suffer.

International support for the sanctions diminished further when it became evident that top officials in Saddam Hussein's government (in particular, Hussein's sons) were profiting from the shortages by hording rationed goods and reselling them for huge profits. The regime also used the distribution of goods to serve its political agenda — for example by withholding food and medical supplies destined for Shi'ite and Kurdish areas as punishment for the post-Gulf War uprisings. According to UN experts, Saddam also smuggled millions of dollars worth of oil through countries like Turkey and Syria and used the money to continue developing Iraq's weapons arsenal.

Although meant to put pressure on Iraq, the embargo also had a detrimental effect on neighboring countries that depended on trade with Iraq for their own economic well-being.

NEOCONS

In the 1970s, a group of leftist liberals grew worried that the United States was was reacting too passively to the threat of attack from the Soviet Union. Their concern led them to adjust their ideologies to the right side of the political spectrum, making them "new conservatives" or "neo-cons."

The neocons (many of them Jewish) were strong supporters of Israel and felt that it was in America's best interest to make sure that the "only functioning democracy in the Middle East" survived and prospered in the midst of radical Islamists.

In addition to protecting Israel, the neocons believe that the United States had a moral responsibility as the most powerful nation on the planet to act as the world's police and to lead the international community toward political enlightenment by developing democracies worldwide. Anything less, they warned, could have catastrophic consequences.

As an example, they pointed to the fateful **Munich Agreement** of 1938 when the British and French allowed **Adolf Hitler** to take over Czechoslovakia as the United States sat idly by. Had the Americans been more involved, they reasoned, the lives of millions of Jewish victims of the Holocaust might have been saved.

Like Hitler, Saddam Hussein had become a totalitarian dictator in the Middle East governing by terror and intimidation. Unlike Hitler, though, Hussein also possessed the near capability to produce nuclear weapons (as was demonstrated by the existence of the **Osirak** nuclear reactor) and, the Neocons believed, was not above passing on those weapons to terrorists.

NEOCONS & THE BUSH ADMINISTRATION	
Dick Cheney	Vice President
Donald Rumsfeld	Secretary of Defense
Paul Wolfowitz	Deputy at the Pentagon
Richard Armitage	Deputy Secretary of State
John Bolton	Undersecretary of State for Disarmament
Richard Perle	Chairman of the Advisory Defense Science Board
Lewis Libby	Asst. to the President and Chief of Staff to VP Cheney

HISTORY

When **Ronald Reagan** became the American President in 1981, the neocons had found a politician who shared their aggressive foreign policy. Men like **Paul Wolfowitz**, **Richard Perle**, **Frank Gaffney** and others joined the Reagan administration and participated in America's confrontation against the U.S.S.R — which, they believed, was responsible for the eventual collapse of the Soviet Empire.

Although Reagan's successor, **George Herbert Walker Bush** ("Bush Senior"), recognized and met the threat of the Baathist regime in Iraq by orchestrating the 1991 Gulf War, neocons believed his decision to allow Saddam to stay in power after the war was a vital and shortsighted mistake – one that cost the lives of hundreds of thousands of Iraqi Shi'ites, Kurds and other opponents and led to the current conflict.

Instead Bush, and his successor, Democratic President **Bill Clinton** (ruled 1993-2001), favored a policy of "containment" through crippling sanctions.

The election in 2000 of **George W. Bush** ("Bush 2"), a conservative Republican, gave the neocons the opportunity to reassert their authority through his administration (see box) in order to push their pro-active agenda.

The terrorist attacks of September 11, 2001demonstrated the cost of complacency against the growing threat of terrorism. It also reinforced the neocons message that the United Stated needed to act immediately and resolutely against rogue nations, specifically Afghanistan and Iraq, -- with or without the backing of the United Nations (which the neocons already felt was an ineffective and antiquated institution) or the endorsement of the international community.

Once a functioning democratic government was installed in Iraq, the neocons reasoned, the whole political dynamics of the Middle East would change. Palestinians, Persians, Syrians, Jordanians and other Arabs, would see the Iraqis enjoying real political, religious and economic freedom and demand the same from their own governments. The Palestinians would come down on the Palestinian Authority (bringing real peace to Israel), the fundamental Shi'a mullahs in Iran would see their authority weaken and other Middle Eastern states would witness rebellions against their corrupt regimes. In the end, democratic, pro-Western governments would pop up all across the traditional Islamic landscape opening up viable economic markets for western products and providing reliable strategic political allies.

ARGUMENTS IN FAVOR OF WAR

1) **Saddam was not fulfilling the promises he made at the end of the Gulf War.**

   a. According to UN Resolution 687, Iraq was obliged to disclose all the details of its programs to develop weapons of mass destruction and ballistic missiles with a range greater than 150 kilometers and all of its holdings of such weapons, their components and production facilities and locations. Instead, Iraq repeatedly obstructed access to sites designated by the UN Special Commission and International Atomic Energy Agency and failed to cooperate with those agencies

2) **Saddam was close to developing nuclear weapons**

   a. According to experts, had Israel not destroyed the capabilities of Iraq's Osirak nuclear facility in 1981, Hussein might have already developed nuclear weapons by the time coalition forces invade in 1991.

3) **Iraq was capable of engaging in chemical and biological warfare**

   a. UN inspectors strongly believed that Iraq maintained stockpiles of chemical agents and Hussein had proven that the regime was willing to use them. Iraqis had used nerve agents Sarin and Tabun as well as mustard gas and cyanide as weapons against Iranian soldiers in 1986 and against the Kurds living in northern Iraq in 1987 and 1988.

4) **Iraq could share weapons with terrorists**

   a. Iraq has had links with international terrorists since the early 1970s including Abu Nidal and Carlos the Jackal. The Bush Administration suspected that Hussein also had ties with al-Qaeda, the terrorist group led by Osama bin Laden believed to be responsible for the September 11 attacks on the United States

5) **Human rights abuses**

   a. Hussein had led a regime of terror since becoming president in 1979 and had used torture and intimidation to keep the population in line.

6) **Sanctions not working**

   a. Hussein's family and high officials profited enormously by smuggling and reselling goods traded in the oil-for-food program that were intended to be distributed to the rest of the population

7) **History of aggression**

   a. Hussein initiated both the war with Iran in 1980 and the Gulf War in 1991 when he invading Kuwait.

8) **Democracy**

   a. A liberated Iraq would kick-start a wave of democratization in the Middle East

ARGUMENTS AGAINST WAR

1) **Containment was successful**
   a. If the United States could contain a superpower like the USSR for more than 40 years, it could continue to contain Iraq successfully.
2) **Iraq was not a direct threat to the United States**
   a. There was no indication that Hussein planned to use weapons of mass destruction against Europe or the United States.
3) **There was no proof that Iraq had nuclear acapabilties**
4) **There was no conclusive evidence that Hussein had any relationship with al-Qaeda or Osama bin Laden.**
   a. In fact, it was unlikely that the fundamental Muslim terrorist groups would associate with Hussein's secular regime.
5) **Little international support**
   a. Regardless of personal antagonisms against Saddam Hussein, Arab countries would feel obliged to defend their fellow-Islamic neighbor.
   b. An unproked invasion of a Muslim country would be considered legitimate grounds for a *jihad* (or "holy war") against the aggressors.
   c. Other countries objected to potential U.S. and British post-war dominance in the region, especially with regards to Iraqi oil.
   d. The war could add fuel to the crisis between Arab countries and the West resulting from the unresolved Israeli-Palestine conflict.
   e. A U.S. invasion of Iraq could destabilize or topple friendly governments in Turkey, Jordan, Egypt, Kuwait and Saudi Arabia.
6) **An attack on Iraq would likely increase the potential for terrorism and actually direct attention away from the war against terrorism.**
7) **Alternatives to war hadn't yet been thoroughly explored.**
   a. Sanctions could have been tightened or done away with altogether.
   b. The West could have lent more support to Iraqi opposition groups
   c. The West could have tried to reduce its dependency on Iraqi oil thereby lessening Iraq's power and influence.
8) **Cost of war and reconstruction.**
   a. Experts believed Britain and the U.S. would have to commit at least $20 billion a year to maintain peace in post-war Iraq and rebuild its infrastructure.
   b. Without allies, the price tag would be overwhelmingly high to U.S. and U.K. taxpayers.
   c. Cost in human lives.
      *By September, 2004, more than 1,000 American soldiers had been killed in Iraq.
9) **Not legal**
   a. According to the UN Charter, the war was not considered "self-defense" and therefore not legal.
10) **A weakened Iraq could be vulnerable to invasion from its neighbors (i.e. Iran) and become a haven for terrorists**

OPERATION IRAQI FREEDOM (OPERATION TELIC)

Saddam Hussein's continued violation of UN resolutions demanding free access for weapons inspectors and the fact that sanctions weren't working provided a solid case for punitive action against the defiant Middle Eastern ruler. After the attacks of September 11, 2001, the case for war escalated even higher when the Western world was suddenly forced to deal with the threat of Islamic terrorism. The assailants in the 2001 attack used planes as weapons, but the next time, it was feared, they could employ weapons of mass destruction or even nuclear bombs that they could get from Iraq.

Saddam Hussein was known to have had contact with terrorists, notably, Palestinian terrorists **Abu Nidal** (murdered in 2002) and **Abu Abbas,** (captured on the outskirts of Baghdad in April 2003), and had already used WMD's on Iranians during the Iran-Iraq War as well as on Shi'as and Kurds in his own country. His resistance to arms inspectors (not allowed in the country since 1998) gave the appearance that he had something to hide and could be concealing nuclear capabilities (confirmed by reports from exiled Iraqi scientists). Add to that his record of human rights abuses and his history of aggression against neighboring states and the argument for his removal by force became overwhelming.

On the other hand, his possession of nuclear arms was never proven (none were found even after troops had invaded the country in 2003) and Iraq did not pose an immediate threat to the United States or any other nation. As a secular and relatively stable country, furthermore, it acted as a bulwark against Iran (which was an even greater threat to U.S. security). In fact, attacking Iraq could stir up a hornet's nest of terrorist activity as Islamic militants swarmed in to defend the country from the Western infidels (as had happened with the arrival of **Abu Musab al-Zarqawi** and his followers). (See Sunni Insurgency p.46).

Furthermore, as the imminent war approached, Saddam Hussein made numerous overtures to the U.S. and the U.N.: for example, by presenting a 12,000 page dossier[6] disclosing Iraq's programs for weapons of mass destruction as demanded by **UN resolution 1441** (see chapter Road to War: UN Resolutions p. 58) and publicly apologizing to the people of Kuwait in December 2003 for invading their country in 1990.

THE ULTIMATUM
In a last ditch attempt to avert war, the United States offered Saddam immunity from prosecution if he left Baghdad (which he refused). Two months later, the U.S. and Britain outlined a series of tasks that the Iraqi dictator should undertake or face war, including: making a public statement admitting that his country possessed WMDs and was willing to give them up;

---

[6] The report was deemed incomplete by **Hans Blix**, the executive chairman of **UNMOVIC,** and other specialists.

making a commitment to allow Iraqi scientists to be interviewed by inspectors outside Iraq; surrendering 10,000 liters of anthrax that he was believed to be holding; and destroying proscribed missiles, remotely piloted vehicles and mobile bio-production laboratories.

Britain, France, Spain and Ireland presented the ultimatum to the United Nations and urged its members to back military action against the rogue nation. In a counterproposal distributed in February 2003 though, France, Germany and Russia argued that war was premature and that

---

THE UN VOTE FOR WAR

A UN Resolution needs 9 out of 15 Security Council votes to pass with no vote against the resolution by any of the 5 permanent members: United States, Britain, France, Russia and China

Votes for resolution proposed by the United States, Britain and Spain authorizing war against Iraq:

("p" = permanent member)

Support	Oppose	Uncertain
Britain (p)	China (p)	Angola
Bulgaria	France (p)	Cameroon
Spain	Germany	Chile
United States (p)	Russia (p)	Guinea
	Syria	Mexico
		Pakistan

---

effective disarmament of Iraq through peaceful means could still be accomplished. Their vetoes sealed the fate of the failed draft resolution forcing Britain, the U.S. and their allies to go it alone – in defiance even of many of their own citizens (who participated in anti-war demonstrations worldwide) and governments (by March 19, 2003, nine members of the British parliament had resigned in protest).

On March 18, 2003, American President **George W. Bush** gave Saddam Hussein 48 hours to leave Iraq or face invasion. The next day, 170,000 coalition troops were massed on the Kuwait border and the war began on March 20, 2003.

OPERATION IRAQI FREEDOM (March 20, 2003 – May 1, 2003)

Because Turkey had refused to allow U.S. troops to deploy from their territory (see chapter on Foreign Relations p. 49), the Americans were forced to enter the country through Kuwait under the command of **General Tommy Franks**. While American troops were making their way to Baghdad, British forces were marching on Basra from the Faw Peninsula in south Iraq. In the north, *peshmerga* fighters penetrated former Kurdish territory that had been "cleansed" of Kurds by the Saddam regime over the past 30 years.

As expected, the coalition forces enjoyed a number of victories within a few days. By April 3rd, U.S. troops captured **Saddam International Airport** (10 miles from Baghdad's city center). Three days later, British troops poured into Basra destroying the Baath party headquarters without a shot being fired. Photographs of U.S. Marines reclining in Saddam's presidential palaces gave the world a glimpse of the opulent lifestyle enjoyed by Saddam and his family while Iraqis suffered from severe deprivation.

Even more poignant and symbolic of the end of the brutal regime were images of Iraqis and U.S. Marines pulling down a giant statue of Saddam Hussein in the heart of Baghdad.

In the north, meanwhile, Kurdish fighters had seized the oil city of Kirkuk causing the Turkish government to become even more concerned that victory would reignite the Kurdish bid for independence.

Saddam's final stronghold, his hometown of Tikrit, fell to coalition forces by mid-April.

With all the key Iraqi cities in Western hands, hostilities were formally ended on May 1, 2003 ushering in the next phase of the war -- the search for infamous Iraqi figures (identified in a pack of playing cards distributed by the U.S. military in April).

The first of the wanted suspects to be captured was Saddam's half-brother, **Barzan Ibrahim al-Tikriti** who was believed to have extensive knowledge of the toppled regime's inner workings. **Tariq Aziz,** Saddam's former deputy prime minister, who had claimed before the war that he would rather die than become an American prisoner, surrendered to U.S. forces in Baghdad on April 24. Saddam's reviled sons **Uday** and **Qusay** (who led Iraq's elite army and security units) were killed in a gun battle in July and **Ali Hassan al-Majid,** also known as **"Chemical Ali,"** the man believed to have ordered the 1988 chemical attack on Kurds, was taken into custody on August 21, 2003.

The biggest prize, **Saddam Hussein**, was captured in December, 2003 when the gaunt and disheveled former leader was found hiding near his home town in a "spider hole" with two AK-47s and $750,000 in U.S. $100 bills.

SETBACKS
With Hussein in custody and Baghdad in the hands of coalition forces, the war had been won – but the aftermath was plagued by violence, insurgency, shortages, scandals, demonstrations and politically damaging revelations about the true status of Iraq's weapons program.

Widespread looting immediately after the war was compounded by shortages of fuel and power. Protests both in Iraq (tens of thousands of Iraqis demonstrated in Baghdad against the US occupation) and at home exhibited continued political condemnation of the war – especially after reports revealed that the US and UK intelligence had made grave mistakes regarding the extent of Iraq's possession of Weapons of Mass Destruction and exaggerated Saddam's links with Al-Qaeda terrorists.

The coalition's ethical justifications for going to war with Iraq, furthermore, was put into question when graphic photos appeared in the media showing American and British guards humiliating Iraqi prisoners at **Abu Ghraib** prison – the kind of abhorrent behavior that the West was ostensibly trying to prevent by shutting down Saddam's brutal regime.

Most disheartening, though, were the prolonged battles between coalition forces and local (and foreign) insurgents within Iraq. (See Shiite Movements and Sunni Insurgency). Iraqi resistance fighters who had rallied around radical Shi'as (particularly **Muqtada al-Sadr**) and violent Sunni groups (especially the group led by **al-Zarqawi**) targeted both soldiers and civilians in their drive to intimidate the invaders into leaving the country. In May, 2004, **Nicholas Berg**, the first in a string of Western hostages, was beheaded by Islamic militants to avenge the abuse of Iraqi detainees by US troops.

IRAQ'S DEBTS

Before the 2003 war, Iraq owed more than $120 billion in commercial debts to foreign banks, companies and governments (in most cases for the purchase of arms). Billions of dollars were also owed for reparations from the 1991 Gulf War to Kuwait and Gulf States. Iraq was also obligated to honor a number of pending contracts – for example, to Russia's Luk Oil which developed Iraqi oil fields in exchange for future shares in profits. The combined debts were the largest of any developing nation amounting to about $16,000 for every man, woman and child in the country or 15 to 20 times Iraq's estimated pre-war annual revenue of $25 billion.

Until 2002, Iraq (which boasts the second largest oil reserves in the world) was typically pumping 1.7 million barrels per day under the UN oil-for-food program, earning between $10 and $15 billion annually. However, even if Iraq was able reactivate and increase its oil producing capabilities, the revenues would still not be enough to pay for the reconstruction of the country (which is predicted to cost about $20 billion a year), let alone pay off its debts.

For that reason, the Americans, who would be saddled with the reconstruction bill, tried to persuade the indebted nations to forgive or reduce the debts owed to them claiming that the new government in Iraq was not responsible for loans or contracts made by the deposed regime (U.S. and U.K. firms were owed little if anything).

Pre-war debt according to the Center for Strategic and International Studies (CSIS): **Total:** *$383 billion* (Sources differ on actual amount)

Pending Contracts: *$57 billion* -- 90% owed to Russia

Foreign Debts: *$127 billion* -- Gulf States - $42b, Kuwait - $17b, Russia $12b (IMB claims $40 b. is owed to members of the Paris Club*)

Gulf War Compensation claims: *$199 billion* -- Kuwait 40%, Jordan 8%, Saudi Arabia 7%, UK 4%, India 4%, Germany 3%

* A group of 19 creditor nations including France, Germany, Russia, Japan, U.K., U.S., Italy, Canada

---

POST-SADDAM GOVERNMENTS

ORHA (Office of Reconstruction and Humanitarian Assistance)
Immediately after the conclusion of the war, coalition forces set up the Office of Reconstruction and Humanitarian Assistance or OSHA under the auspices of the U.S. Defense Department. Headed by **Jay Garner**, who was answerable to U.S. War Commander **General Tommy Franks**, the organization was charged with providing humanitarian assistance, developing civil administration and coordinating reconstruction of post-Saddam Iraq. Along with preparing the way for the creation of a democratic Iraqi-run government, the organization was prepared to overhaul everything from the country's currency (which featured Hussein's portrait) to the country's legal code, schools, police service and utilities.

OSHA consisted of a core staff of about twelve people supplemented by "free Iraqis" – that is, Iraqis who had been living in the U.S. or Europe with no affiliations to particular Iraqi opposition groups.

The organization was finally replaced by the Coalition Provisional Authority in May, 2003 because of the controversial background of its leader, Jay Garner, who had once signed a statement supporting Israel,[7] and the incompetence of its personnel.

COALITION PROVISIONAL GOVERNMENT (CPA) (May 12, 2003 –June 28, 2004)
On May 12, 2003, **Paul Bremer**, a former counter-terrorism expert at the U.S. State Department, took the post of Iraq's new civil administrator overseeing the Coalition Provisional Authority (CPA). Immediately after taking power, Bremer created a new U.S.-trained Iraqi police forced, began the process of De-Baathification and set up an Iraqi Special Tribunal to try Iraqi residents accused of genocide or crimes against humanity committed between 1968 and 2003.

Bremer's drive to root out all people with any association to the Baath party (including disbanding Iraq's military) left hundreds of thousands of Iraqi citizens without jobs and left few competent administrators to serve in Iraq's interim government. The de-Baathification policy was slowly reversed out of necessity but not before steering many discontented and armed former soldiers into militant organizations.

IRAQI GOVERNING COUNCIL (in Arabic, Majilis al-Hukm) (July 13, 2003 – June 2004)
A month after its creation, the Coalition Provisional Authority appointed the Iraqi Governing Council, a temporary Iraqi governing body subordinated to the CPA. Administrators to the diverse 25-member council were chosen by

---

[7] Some Iraqis believe that the U.S. invaded Iraq to protect Israel and think that Israel and the US have been conspiring to divide up the Arab world.

the US-led coalition on the basis of population numbers. Hence the body consisted of 13 Shi'a Muslims, 5 Sunni Muslims, 5 Kurds, 1 Christian Assyrian and 1 Turkman (no Baathists). Among the members three were women. Nine of the Council members served as president for a month in a rotating presidential term established on July 28, 2003 – the first being **Ibrahim Jaafari,** a Shiite spokesman for the Islamic **Da'wa Party** (see chapter on Shiite Movements) who served from August 1-August 31, 2003.

Among the members of the Council:

Ahmad Chalabi

Former exile and leader of the London-based Iraqi National Council (INC) (see box)
Chalabi fell from grace when it was discovered that he provided flawed intelligence to the U.S.

Abdul Aziz al-Hakim (see chapter Shiite Movements)

Hakim and his brother, Muhammad Baqir al-Hakim, returned to Iraq from Iran after 20 years of exile. After his brother was killed in 2003, Abdul Aziz became the leader of SCIRI.

Massoud Barzani and Jalal Talabani

Leaders of the two main Kurdish groups (see chapter on Kurds)
Massoud Barzani heads the Kurdistan Democratic Party (KDP) founded in 1946 by his father.
Talabani heads the Patriotic Union of Kurdish (PUK) a breakaway Kurdish party founded in 1957.

Adnan Pachachi

The strongest representative of the non-Kurdish Sunni minority, former foreign minister, Pachachi set up and headed the Iraqi Independent Democrats Movement in February 2003.

Iyad Allawi

Medical doctor, long-time oppositionist and future Prime Minister of the Iraqi Interim Government (see below), Iyad Allawi headed the Iraqi National Accord Party.

Aqilah al-Hashimi

One of 3 women on the 25-member governing council, Hashimi was shot to death in September 2003 by Iraqi insurgents targeting Iraqis collaborating with the U.S.-led administration in Iraq.

Ibrahim Jaafari (Ja'afari)

Spokesman for the Islamic Da'wa Party. Jaafari was later appointed one of two Vice Presidents in the Iraqi Interim Government.

Ezzedine Salim

A leader in a breakaway faction of the Da'wa party, Salim was killed in a bombing in May 2004 while he held a position in the rotating presidency of the Governing Council.

The Council was responsible for securing stability and security in the country, delivering public services and reviving the economy. It was also charged with the creation of an interim constitution or **"Transitional Administrative Law"** (signed on March 8, 2004) which would provide the framework for the future sovereign Iraqi government.

INTERIM IRAQI GOVERNMENT (IIG) (June 28, 2004 – 2005)

The CPA and 25-member Governing Council dissolved two days ahead of schedule on June 28, 2004 to be replaced by the autonomous Interim Iraqi Government. By transferring power early, the occupation forces hoped to catch insurgents off-guard and avert any planned sabotage campaigns.

The new government was sworn in on the Quran in a small ceremony in the well-guarded Green Zone. After shaking hands with the new Prime Minister, **Iyad Allawi**, the U.S. proconsul **Paul Bremer** boarded a plane and flew home. In his place, **John Negroponte** was appointed as the new ambassador of the largest U.S. embassy in the world.

The IIG was expected to serve as a caretaker government until elections conducted around January 2005. The transitional government was led by a prime minister who was charged with overseeing governmental administration, a president who would act as Head of State in a largely ceremonial position, two vice presidents and 26 appointed ministers. A consultative assembly was elected in August, 2004 with 25% of the seats being allotted to women.

Once in power, the IIG accepted responsibility for more than 6,000 Iraqi prisoners including Saddam Hussein. The IIG also had full control over foreign relations, natural resources (including oil) and international financial negotiations. Although the new government was allowed a single armed division of 8,000 soldiers, security largely remained the responsibility of the coalition forces. Opposition militia groups were all banned by Allawi (including the Badr brigade, which changed its name to the **Badr Organization for Development and Reconstruction.**, the al-**Mahdi Army**). The Kurdish *Peshmerga* units were not immediately disbanded since they were necessary for maintaining security in northern Iraq.

While the IIG was nominally sovereign, Allawi's independent authority was doubted by many opponents who maintained that the IIG and Allawi were merely puppets of the coalition forces. Allawi's credibility would have been greatly enhanced if he demanded the complete withdrawal of the Western/Christian forces. However, the fledgling interim government depended on coalition military services for security and American financial aid for reconstruction (the U.S. Congress promised to provide $18.4 billion dollars for Iraq's reconstruction).

Rotating presidency of the Iraq Governing Council

Ibrihim Jaafari	8/1/03	–	8/31/03	DIP, Shiite
Ahmad Chalabi	9/1/03	–	9/30/03	INC, Shiite
Iyad Allawi	10/1/03	–	10/31/03	INA, Shiite
Jalal Talabani	11/1/03	–	11/30/03	PUK, Sunni Kurd
Abdul Aziz al-Hakim	12/1/03	–	12/31/03	SCIRI, Shiite
Adnan Pachachi	1/1/04	–	1/31/04	n/p, Sunni
Muhsin Abd al-Hamid	2/1/04	–	2/29/04	IIP, Sunni
Muhammad al-Ulum	3/1/04	–	3/31/04	n/p, Shiite
Massoud Barzani	4/1/04	–	4/30/04	KDP, Sunni Kurd
Ezzedine Salim	5/1/04	–	5/17/04	DIP, Shiite
Ghazi al-Yawar	5/17/04	–	6/1/04	n/p, Sunni

DIP (Da'wa Islamic Party), INC (Iraqi National Congress), INA (Iraqi National Accord), PUK (Patriotic Union of Kurdistan), SCIRI (Supreme Council for the Islamic Revolution in Iraq), IIP (Iraqi Islamic Party), KDP (Kurdistan Democratic Party).

IRAQI NATIONAL CONGRESS (INC)

The INC was formed in 1992 when two main Kurdish factions, the KDP headed by Massoud Barzani and the PUK headed by Jalal Talabani, decided to attend a meeting in Vienna comprising nearly 200 delegates from dozens of Iraqi opposition groups. Four months later, the major Shiites groups joined the coalition in another meeting in northern Iraq. The INC appointed a 3-man leadership council and a 26-member Executive council led by chairman **Ahmad Chalabi**, an Iraqi Shiite who had founded the Jordanian Petra Bank (Chalabi was later convicted for embezzlement by the Jordanian government). The INC program complemented the US agenda in Iraq including the establishment of human rights and the rule of law and the creation of a constitutional, democratic and pluralistic government. The INC was heavily funded by the CIA receiving over $100 million in the first half of the 1990s in hopes that it could one day act as an alternative government to Saddam's Baathist regime with Chalabi as interim president. However, internal differences rendered it ineffective and Chalabi fell out of favor with the Americans when it was discovered that he had provided false intelligence and was a corrupt, self-serving and unpopular figure among many elements in Iraq.

KURDS

Records of the Kurds existence in Mesopotamia reach as far back as 3000 B.C. From the time they were first mentioned in cuneiform writing in the time of the Sumerians (as people who came from the "land of the Kardas,") Kurds have enjoyed a certain degree of autonomy because of the inaccessibility of the area they live in (which is surrounded by high mountains) and their fighting skills.

The Kurds are a non-Arabic, primarily Sunni Muslim group of people who speak a language related to Persian (the language spoken in Iran). Traditionally they were nomadic herders organized into a number of tribal and family groups. Although today they are associated with a region called "Kurdistan," (which spans across parts of Iraq, Iran and Turkey), the term more accurately denotes their cultural and linguistic distinction. As drifters, the Kurds originally saw no need to identify with any particular geographic area until WWI and the consequent breakup of the Ottoman Empire forced them to live within artificially designated borders.

When the British initially created Iraq from the *vilayets* of Baghdad and Basra in 1916, they hadn't yet decided what to do with the Kurds living in the Ottoman Empire's former *vilayet* of Mosul (in northern Iraq). Like other ethnic groups at the time, the Kurds petitioned for independence after World War I and were granted their own country of Kurdistan in the **Treaty of Sevres**, the 1920 treaty that divided the Ottoman Empire into the modern states of Syria, Iraq and Kuwait. But the agreement was overturned by the Turks under **Mustafa Kemal Ataturk**, and by other countries who jointly decided not to recognize an independent Kurdish state that would take territory away from their own countries.

At the same time, the British were interested in maintaining control over a portion of the Kurdish territories after it was discovered that the region had vast oil deposits. The **Treaty of Lausanne** (which superseded the Treaty of Sevres in 1923), divided Kurdistan among the countries around its borders and place the oil-rich Mosul region within British-run Iraq.

After 1923, "Kurdistan" and the Kurdish population were divided among the new states of Iraq (where about four million Kurds now lived making up 23% of Iraq's population), Turkey (11 million Kurds and 19% of Turkey's population), Iran (five million Kurds, 10% of Iran's population), Syria (one million Kurds, 8% of the population) and smaller communities lived in Armenia. Hence, the Kurds had become the largest minority group in the Middle East.

Working together, the militant Kurds might have eventually succeeded in securing their own independent state. However, strong tribal and clan loyalties kept the Kurds fractured. Turkish Kurds fought Iraqi Kurds, for example, and the Iraqi Kurds were split into competing cliques.

Kurds in Iraq

One of the most prominent Iraqi Kurd groups, the **Kurdish Democratic Party** (KDP), was founded in 1946 as a political party after World War II by **Mustafa Barzani**, in opposition to British influence. When the monarchy was overthrown in 1958, the KDP supported the new republican government of **Abdul Karim Kassim** whose regime, in turn, granted the Kurds a number of liberties including the right to publish books and periodicals in their language, broadcast news in Kurdish, and use Kurdish as the language of instruction in schools.

But the rights were revoked a couple of years later when the **Baathists** attempted to destabilize and weaken the Kurds through a campaign of "**Arabization**" and forced integration. The Kurds (aroused by the KDP), sharply resisted the Baathist's campaign, turning the conflict into a prolonged battle between the Iraqi troops and the Kurds under **Barzani**.

In 1974, the Kurds turned to Iran for weapons and support in their battle of resistance against Iraq's military. But they were crushed when the Persians (under the **Shah**) promised Iraq that they would withdraw support from the Kurds in return for control of the **Shatt-al-Arab** waterway (the **Algiers Agreement**, see section on Iran-Iraq War). Without Iran's support, the Baathists were free to launch a devastating attack on the Kurds killing thousands of Kurdish fighters, forcing some 130,000 Kurds into Iran and effectively extinguishing the resistance. Barzani, like many of the Kurdish fighters, fled to the United States, where he died in 1979.

The resistance was taken up again by another Kurdish nationalist, **Jalal Talabani**, under the banner of the **Patriotic Union of Kurdistan (PUK)** in 1976. Talabani's radical splinter group led the Kurdish struggle from bases inside Iraq during the 1980s, further frustrating Iraq's military action against Iran and its Islamic Revolutionary leader **Ayatollah Khomeini** (see chapter on Iran-Iraq War p. 14).

At the war's end in 1988, Saddam Hussein hoped to finally eliminate the Kurdish "problem" altogether by razing hundreds of Kurdish villages in northern Iraq and killing hundreds of thousands of people in poison gas attacks in retaliation for Kurdish rebellion. In one of the most brutal of the chemical attacks collectively known as the "**Anfal**" campaign, Iraqi military bombers dropped missiles filled with a cocktail of chemical weapons that instantly killed thousands of Kurdish men, women and children in the border city of **Halabja**. Under orders from Hussein's cousin, **Ali Hassan al-Majid** ("**Chemical Ali**" – captured by Americans in August 2003) the attacks continued from February to September 1988.

In 1990, in anticipation of Iraq's defeat by the United States and allied forces (see "Gulf War"), the main Iraqi Kurdish parties (the **KDP** was now under the command of Barzani's sons), negotiated with Shi'ite dissidents to create a united front with the common goal of overthrowing Hussein and setting up a coalition government. Although the merger wasn't accomplished, both groups rebelled against the Iraqi regime after the March 1991 cease-fire, expecting the United States to support the uprising.

When Western aid didn't come, Hussein freely orchestrated another wave of repression against dissidents involved in the three-week anti-government insurrections. Thousands of unarmed civilians were executed for their activities and tens of thousands of civilians were arrested or deported.

In northern Iraq, Kurds tried to escape the onslaught by fleeing to border countries, Iran and Turkey While more than a million were accepted into Iran, Kurds amassing on the Turkish border met a different fate. The refugees were refused entry by the Turkish government and found themselves stranded in the wintry mountains without food or shelter. Thousands of Kurds died from exposure and hunger before the United States implemented **Operation Provide Comfort** – a project designed to make the

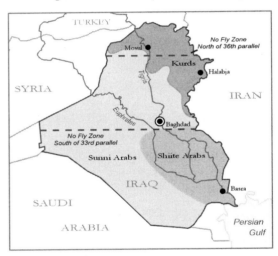

Kurdish people feel safe enough to leave Turkey and resettle in their own homeland. Camps were set up with relief supplies and western troops patrolled the area. In April, 1991, the U.S., Britain and France imposed the "**no-fly zone**" which prohibited Iraqi planes from flying above the 36 degrees parallel.

Under foreign protection, the Iraqi Kurdish community flourished. By 1992, the Kurds established an "autonomous region" in Northern Iraq and held general elections. Initially, power in the newly established regional government was shared by the two main Kurdish parties (the **PUK** and **KDP**). After about four years of fighting (which, at one point, required intervention by Baghdad and other countries), the parties decided to divide the area into spheres of influence with the KDP (under **Massoud Barzani**) controlling the western region, the PUK (led by chief **Jalal Talbani**) based in Sulaymaniyah controlling the south-eastern part of Iraqi Kurdistan and the central government in charge of the south.

In the years before the 2003 war, the Kurds enjoyed unprecedented freedoms and civil liberties. Hundreds of newspapers and magazines were published in Kurdish and other languages in the main cities, internet access was unfettered and satellite dishes abounded. Turkoman, Assyrians and other minorities living in the area had their own political parties and participated in the democratic government.

Moreover, Iraqi "Kurdistan" had profited from commercial transit of legal and illegal goods through the area (particularly cheap oil). The Kurds also received a greater share of humanitarian items purchased under the oil-for-food program than other Iraqis.

Despite the assertion by the Iraqi Kurds that they were not interested in establishing a greater "Kurdistan," the "era of self-rule" and comparative wealth had raised concern in Turkey and Iran. Fearing that the region could become a base for separatist Kurds in their own countries, Turkey and Iran considered Iraqi Kurd sovereignty to be a potential threat to their own national security and internal stability.

- Kurdish dominated areas
  smaller areas not shown

200 Kilometers
200 Miles

With hostile nations neighboring on all its borders, the Kurds couldn't afford to lose Western protection. But the history of former allies withdrawing support without notice made dependence on foreign aid particularly daunting to the Kurds.

Since the war in Iraq was officially declared over on May 1, 2003 tens of thousands of Iraqi Kurds returned to lands they once occupied in the north of the country. But critics say the returning Kurds are now forcing out Arabs who were brought in by Saddam Hussein to resettle the area as part of the regime's Arabization campaign.

Much of the tension is centered on the oil-rich city of **Kirkuk**, long considered the heart and soul of the Kurdish people where the Kurds have been accused of discriminating against Arabs.

MARSH ARABS

In a remote region at the confluence of the Tigris and Euphrates rivers lived a notable group of Shi'ites, the **Ma'dan** or Marsh Arabs. For centuries this ancient community was almost untouched by the civilizations that came through Mesopotamia and maintained their unique culture based on traditional occupations of fishing, buffalo breeding and reed gathering. But the same isolation that protected the Ma'dan from invaders also made it attractive to Shia rebels looking for refuge from the Iraqi regime.

For this reason, and because the area had some of the richest oil deposits in the country, the Marsh Arabs were particularly singled out for repression after the Shi'ite uprisings in 1991. Thousands of Ma'dan were arrested, tortured, executed and forced to migrate, shrinking the population from about 400,000 inhabitants in the 1950s to less that 20,000 today. To facilitate entry into the area by the armed forces, moreover, the marshlands were drained – destroying one of the largest wetland ecosystems in the world.

The dams that had turned the marshland into barren desert were ultimately torn down after U.S. forces invaded Iraq in 2003, slowly returning the region to its former lush state. But though living conditions and security improved significantly as a result, the Marsh Arabs continue to live in poverty without schools, hospitals or even clean drinking water.

TURKOMAN (TURKMEN)

The Turkoman make up the third largest ethnic group in Iraq after the Kurds and Arabs. Most of the nearly 2,000,000 Turkomans in Iraq live in the Kirkuk and Mosul Provinces and compete with the Kurds for control of the territories. Like the Kurds, the Turkoman were victims of the Baath party's drive to Arabacize the Iraqi population by prohibiting the use of the Turkoman language in schools, the government and even on public street, and relocating Turkoman out of their cities and moving Arabs in.

Since they share cultural and linguistic ties to Turkey (Turkomans speak an Oguz-Turkic language) they have played an important role in the political relationship between the western coalition forces and Turkey – who have championed the cause of the Turkomans.

The Turkoman, which had been omitted as an ethnic minority in Iraq's 1990 constitution, were allotted a seat in the Iraqi Governing Council of 2003.

ASSYRIANS

The Assyrians are descendants of the ancient empires of Assyria and Babylonia which once ruled over Mesopotamia. Most Assyrians are Christian following the Chaldean church, Syriac Orthodox church and the Church of the East. They suffered brutal opression under Saddam Hussein because of their ethnicity and religion (Christians were required to adopt Muslim names). Assyrians were allotted a seat in the IGC.

SHI'ITES

Iraq is one of only three countries in the world that has a Shi'ite majority (the other two are Bahrain and Iran) and it is home to Shi'ism's most sacred shrines. Even Baghdad, Iraq's capital, has a population that is primarily Shi'ite. But in politics, the Shi'ites have been terribly underrepresented. Saddam Hussein and his Tikriti Sunni-Muslim regime ruled the religious majority with a heavy hand by imprisoning Shi'ite men, assassinating popular clerics, by deporting thousands of Shi'ite women and children to Iran and keeping the southern part of Iraq (where most Shi'ites live) in a state of poverty that was unmatched in the rest of the country.

The split between the two Muslim groups (Shi'ites and Sunnis) began soon after the **Prophet Muhammad's** death in A.D. 632. The Shi'a or *Shi'at Ali* ("Party of Ali") believed that the prophet's cousin and son-in-law, **Ali ibn Abi Talib,** was Muhammad's rightful successor (caliph) but the Muslim community chose the Prophet's close friend and supporter, **Abu Bakr**, to lead the Muslims instead. After Bakr's death (and the death of two more caliphs after him) Ali was finally appointed to lead the Muslim population as the fourth caliph in A.D. 656. Five years later, though, Ali was assassinated and the Caliphate passed to his son, **Hassan** – but not without a fight.

Also vying for the position was **Mu'awiya**, the governor of Damascus, who forced Hassan to abdicate six months after his appointment and took the position of fifth caliph himself. When Mu'awiya died, his son, **Yazin**, took the position, which outraged many Muslims because of his excessive drinking and wasteful lifestyle. Some disenchanted followers called on **Hussein**, Hassan's brother and Muhammad's youngest grandson, to retake power from the usurper Yazin.

In a celebrated battle in the city of **Karbala** (in present-day Iraq), Hussein and the Shi'ite rebels fought Yazin's forces valiantly until Hussein and his troops were massacred. Hussein's martyrdom on the battlefield became on of the most momentous events in the history of Shi'ism and the pilgrimages to Karbala and the Iraqi city of **Najaf** (the burial site of Ali, the fourth caliph) became a regular ritual from that point on.

Although Iraq was the spiritual center of Shi'ism in the 16th century (housing the most holy Shi'a Muslim sights), Persia (present-day Iran) acted as its administrative base after **Ismail I**, the Shah of Persia and leader of the Safavid movement, established Shi'ism as the state religion.

For centuries, Iraq became a battleground between the Shi'ites of Persia and the Sunnis of the Ottoman Empire, with Shi'ites living in Basra (in southern

Iraq) stuck in the middle. When ruled by the Persians, Shi'ites lived favorably in Basr, when the Sunnis ruled they suffered (as they did under the Sunni Baathist regime).

When the British came to power in the 1920s, things didn't get much better. The Shi'ites were treated with distrust by the British, who decided to install a Sunni government in Iraq in deference to the Sunni Arab nations that had supported the British in World War I, and they were virtually shut out of the puppet governments of Saudi King Faisal and his successors. Only five out of thirty Iraqi prime minister who ruled from 1921 until the end of the monarchy in 1958, were Shi'ite, the rest were Sunni. The Baathists continued the trend.

The Baathist party had always equated Iraqi Shi'ites with Persians, although the two were ethnically very different. Shi'ite Muslims in Iraq were Arabic while Persian Shi'ites were, well, Persian (Persians may also be Sunnis or even Christians and Jews). Both groups practiced the religion in slightly different ways and had unique cultural characteristics.

Nevertheless, the Baath regime deported more than 100,000 Shi'ites from Iraq to Iran in the 1970s (to diminish their numbers and influence), and became particularly uneasy about Shi'ites loyalty during the war with Iran in the 1980s.

Since 1965, the exiled Shi'ite **Ayatollah Khomeini**, Iran's eventual spiritual leader, had been living in the Iraqi city of Najaf. When the Shah asked the Iraqis to expel him in 1978, the Baathists happily obliged, fearing that Khomeini was fomenting discontent among Iraqi Shi'ites in the area. But Khomeini gathered an even bigger following from his new home in Paris, France. By the time the Shah had been kicked out of Iran, Khomeini had won enough support to step in and lead a revolution.

The turn of events terrified Sunni Iraqis. Tehran was only a two-day drive from Baghdad and Iraq's army was largely composed of Shi'ite soldiers. If the new wave of Shi'ite fundamentalism aroused Iraq's Shi'ites, more importantly, there could be a devastating rebellion. With Persian help, moreover, the uprising could topple the ruling regime and wipe out Iraq altogether. None of those things happened but the threat was dire enough to compel Saddam Hussein to take extreme measures against the potential insurgents.

After a possibly staged assassination attempt against Saddam's foreign affairs advisor, **Tariq Aziz**, by Shi'a fanatics (members of the Shi'ite resistance group, Da'wa), Hussein had a good excuse to crack down on the community. More than 100,000 people were imprisoned or deported to Iran in retaliation for the assassination attempt. Another half a million were expelled over the course of the 1980s under suspicions that they were sympathetic to or collaborating with Iran.

Along with deportations, the Iraqi regime tortured and killed a number of Shi'ite clerics in order to deprive the Shi'ites of capable rulers and to scare other leaders into submission, and passed discriminatory legislation against the Islamic groups. Shi'ite holy sites were desecrated, mosques, libraries and centers of learning were closed, Shi'ite religious rites and practices were restricted and printed materials were censored. The tactics worked and the Iran-Iraq war ended without a Shi'ite rebellion.

After the Gulf War in 1991, though, the Shi'ites were galvanized to rise up against the regime – in part because they believed Saddam was no longer in power after the military defeat and assumed that the West would back them.

Initially, the revolt that had been encouraged by then-president George H.W. Bush (Bush Sr.) was successful. Within weeks after the war's end, 15 of 18 Iraqi provinces were under the control of Shi'ite or Kurd rebels. The West, though, wasn't ready to commit to a lengthy, uncertain and costly campaign to reconstruct Iraq's government after the existing regime was overthrow and did not support the insurgents.

Saddam's Republican Guards easily retook the rebel towns one by one and unleashed a brutal and punishing wave of repression. Thousands of unarmed Shi'ite civilians were killed in numerous cities for their purported participation in the insurgency and assassinations of prominent religious leaders resumed, sparking more demonstrations and, subsequently, more arrests and executions.

The physical oppression was eased after the United Nations imposed a "no-fly zone" at the 32 degree latitude, but as long as the Sunni Baathists controlled the distribution of rationed goods, the Shi'a got the short end of the stick. Iraqi government media accounts used the dire situation in southern Iraq as propaganda to show the rest of the world how much misery the persistent embargo had caused in Iraq.

The Shi'ites (55% of Iraq's population) remained a formidable force in Iraq and constituted the greatest potential threat to Saddam's grip on power.

SHI'A TERMS

SADR FAMILY
Grand Ayatollah Syed[8] Mohammed Baqir al-Sadr (1934? – 1980)
Founded the Da'wa Islamic Party in the late 1950s. Executed by Saddam Hussein's regime in 1980.

Grand Ayatollah Mohammed Sadiq al-Sadr (1943? – 1999)
Baqir al-Sadr's cousin. Assassinated with his two eldest sons in 1999. Father of Muqtada al-Sadr.

Muqtada al-Sadr (1974? -)
Baqir al-Sadr's son. Head of the al-Mahdi Army.

HAKIM FAMILY
Grand Ayatollah Syed Muhsin Al-Hakim (? – 1971)
Worldwide leader of Shi'a Muslims from 1955-1970

Ayatollah Syed Muhammad Baqir al-Hakim (1939 – 2003)
Son of Muhsin al-Hakim
Founded SCIRI (Supreme Council for Islamic Revolution in Iraq)
Killed August 2003

Syed Abdul Aziz al-Hakim (1959 -)
Ayatollah Muhammad Baqir al-Hakim's brother
Took over as leader of SCIRI after his death in 2003

KHOEI FAMILY
Grand Ayatollah Syed Abu al-Qasim al-Khoei (1899-1992)
Made the most prominent Grand Ayatollah in 1971 after the death of Grand Ayatollah Muhsin Sayid Al-Hakim

Syed Abdul Majid al-Khoei (1963 – 2003)
Son of Abu al-Qasim al-Khoei
Assassinated in Najaf in April 2003 by Muqtaqa al-Sadr's followers.

GRAND AYATOLLAH SYED ALI AL-SISTANI
Sistani is widely regarded as the spiritual leader of Iraq's Shi'a Muslims.

DA'WA (Daawa)
Founded in the 1950s, Da'wa is the oldest of the Shi'a Islamist movements. The party's spokesman, **Ibrahami al-Jaafari**, participated in the Iraqi Governing Council. A senior member of Da'wa, **Ezzedine Salim,** was assassinated in May 2004 while he was serving as one of the rotating presidents in the Council.

SCIRI
An umbrella movement of Shi'ite activists formed in Iran in 1982 by Ayatollah Syed Muhammad Baqir al-Hakim dedicated to the overthrow of

---

[8]The attribute "Syed" indicates that the family is a direct descendent of the Prophet Muhammed through his daughter Fatima and cousin/son-in-law Ali.

Hussein's regime. At one point, Da'wa was one of its constituent organizations but the two groups developed a deadly rivalry by the 1990s.

BADR BRIGADE

Armed wing of SCIRI renamed the Badr Organization for Development and Reconstruction after coalition officials banned party militias in September, 2003.

SADR CITY

A slum of 2 million Iraqis in East Baghdad. After the fall of Saddam Hussein's regime in 2003, the city was renamed Sadr City (from Saddam City) after its local hero, the **Grand Ayatollah Mohammed Sadiq al-Sadr.**

MAHDI

Shi'ite Muslims believe that the Prophet Muhammed's successors came from a line of descendants from Muhammed's cousin and son-in-law, Ali, and his wife, the Prophet's daughter, **Fatima. Twelver** Shia's (the Shi'ite branch observed by the majority of Shi'ite Muslims in Iran and Iraq) follow the line through 11 successors or "Imams." They believe the last or 12th Imam (hence the name "Twelvers") disappeared into a supernatural realm and will return to prepre the way for the second coming of **Jesus** ("Isa" in Arabic) and the impending end of the world.

AL-MAHDI ARMY The militia loyal to Muqtada al-Sadr.

NAJAF (An Najaf)

An Islamic holy city south of Baghdad.

The city is the home of the shrine of **Imam Ali ibn Abi Talib**, Prophet Muhammed's cousin and son-in-law (married to Muhammed's daughter Fatima).

It is also the sight of the most sacred Shi'a Islamic cemetery. Shi'a Muslims believe that if they are buried here (near the tomb of Ali) they will enter paradise.

Najaf was considered the center of Shi'ite seminary education before Saddam Hussein conducted mass arrests and expelled senior clerics (the city of Qom in Iran became the temporary center). The importance of Najaf as a hub of Islamic scholarship was restored after Saddam's fall in mid-2003 when scores of clerics returned to the city.

During his 12-year exile, the Grand Ayatollah Ruhollah Khomeini lived in Najaf where he prepared to lead the 1979 revolution in Iran.

AYATOLLAH Senior-most of Shi'a spiritual leaders (see ranking sidebar).

OBJECT OF EMULATION

The most popular Shi'ite clergyman – usually the foremost scholar in the shrine and seminary city of Najab. In the 1960s, the Object of Emulation was Grand Ayatollah Muhsin Syed al-Hakim. After his death in 1971, the title was passed to **Grand Ayatollah Syed Abu al-Qasim al-Khoei.**

SHI'ITE MOVEMENTS

HISTORY OF THE DA'WA PARTY

One of the oldest of the Shi'a political parties in Iraq was founded in 1957 by **Muhammad Baqir al-Sadr** to establish an Islamic state in Iraq. The party was repressed by the Baathists after the Islamic Revolution in Iran in 1979 and in response to Shi'ite demonstrations. Its founder, Baqir al-Sadr was hanged by Saddam's forces in 1980 and being a member of the Dawa party was made a capital crime. After many of its members were arrested by Saddam's regime, the party went underground and split into several factions. Iraqi Shi'ites exiled to Iran developed an Iran-based Da'wa and others joined the party in London where they enjoyed great freedom of movement. Members of the Da'wa party who remained in southern Iraq suffered mass arrests and executions under the Baathist regime especially after the post-Gulf War uprisings in 1991.

After Saddam's regime was defeated in 2003, the party was re-integrated in Iraq and participated in the coalition-led Iraqi Governing Council and the interim government established in June 2004. Despite the return of members from Iran and London, the party remains fragmented and has lost some support because of Da'wa's cooperation with the occupying forces

SUPREME COUNCIL FOR ISLAMIC REVOLUTION IN IRAQ (SCIRI)

One of the foremost opponents of Saddam's regime was **Ayatollah Muhammad Baqir al-Hakim** who founded a political group called the **Islamic Movement** in the late 1960s with the **Ayatollah Muhammad Baqir al-Sadr**. Like Sadr, al-Hakim spent much of his life in jail for his opposition to the Baathist party.

In 1980, al-Hakim left Iraq for Iran where he established the **Supreme Council of the Islamic Resistance in Iraq** (SCIRI) which engaged in political activity against Saddam's regime from its Persian base. In 1991, he assumed his father's role as leader of Iraqi Shi'as, (his father, **Grand Ayatollah Muhsin al-Hakim** was a worldwide leader of Shia Muslims from 1955 to 1970) and in 2003, he was elevated to Grand Ayatollah.

At the end of hostilities in Iraq, Al-Hakim ended his 23-year exile by returning to his homeland with the military arm of SCIRI, the **Badr Brigade**. With the backing of his Iranian trained and financed 10,000-strong militia, Hakim became one of the most influential Iraqi leaders supporting the Iraqi Governing Council.

In part because of his support for the occupiers and his Iranian backing, Ayatollah Hakim was killed in a massive car bombing in Najaf in August 2003 along with 75 other people. It remained unclear who was behind the attack. Some analysts believed Saddam Hussein loyalists were behind the assassination: others believed Hakim's killers were Sunnis opposed to Shi'a influence or came from competing Shi'a groups, such as followers of the young radical Shi'a cleric, Muqtada al-Sadr (see below).

Ayatollah Hakim's brother, **Syed Abdul Aziz al-Hakim** took over as leader of the SCIRI and the Badr Brigade and served as a Interim President of the Iraqi Governing Council in December 2003.

ABU AL-QASIM AL-KHOEI

After the death of **Grand Ayatollah Muhsin al-Hakim** in 1971, the role of **Object of Emulation** (the most popular Shi'ite clergyman was passed to **Abu al-Qasim al-Khoei**. Like many of his fellow Shi'ites, the Grand Ayatollah was arrested after the Gulf War and placed under house arrest.

After his death in 1992, the Shi'as were split in their allegiances between the older generation who followed Khoei's disciple, the **Grand Ayatollah Ali Sistani**, and the younger generation who were drawn to the younger activist scholar **Muhammad Sadiq al-Sadr**.

Khoei's son, **Abd al Majid al-Khoei**, meanwhile, lived in exile in London where he secured the trust of the Americans and British who saw him as the great moderate hope among Shi'ite clerics. With funding from the U.S. government, he returned to Iraq in April 2003 to assume a leadership role.

GRAND AYATOLLAH ALI SISTANI

After the death of **Grand Ayatollah Abu al-Qasim al-Khoei**, many Iraqi Shi'ite Muslims recognized the spiritual leadership of his disciple, the **Grand Ayatollah Ali Sistani**. Born in the Iranian holy city of Qom and educated in Najaf, Iraq, **Sistani** was influenced by his mentor, al-Khoei, and adopted his conviction that religion and politics shouldn be mixed. By keeping a low profile in the political sphere, he was able to survive Saddam Hussein's repression against Iraqi Shi'ites and develop a strong theological base of supporters.

When the U.S.-led forces invaded Iraq, Sistani continued to keep his distance from the conflict and urged his followers to do the same by not taking arms against the occupation force. From the first month after the war, Sistani was courted by the West because of his moderate views, even after the cleric criticized U.S. political decisions (he has called for direct elections) and his open ambition to impose an Islamic identity on post-Saddam Iraq.

As Ayatollah, Ali-Sistani is in charge of millions of dollars donated by Muslims worldwide to pay for the religious education of future Islamic scholars and exerts great authority over the Shi'a population.

GRAND AYATOLLAH MUHAMMAD SADIQ AL-SADR

While many of the older, conservative Shi'a Muslims followed Sistani's religious leadership after the death of the senior Khoei in 1992, the younger Shi'ites chose to assemble around the fiery young cleric, **Ayatollah Muhammad Sadiq al-Sadr**, cousin of the martyred Islamic theorist, **Muhammad Baqir al-Sadr**.

Sadr and his loyal followers — most from the slums of East Baghdad ("Sadr City") where Sadr had established charitable institutions and a network of mosques — were vocal opponents of Saddam Hussein and often rioted against the Baathist regime (particularly in 1977 and 1991). Sadr's boldness eventually led to his assassination by Saddam's secret police in 1999.

MUQTADA AL-SADR
Muhammed Sadiq al-Sadr's son, **Muqtada al-Sadr**, took over where his father had left off, though in his late 20s, the younger Sadr lacked the religious training required of the highest-ranking Shi'ite leaders. Instead, Muqtada al-Sadr based his authority on his lineage which included his father, the martyred Shi'ite cleric **Ayatollah Sadiq al-Sadr** and his uncle, the **Ayatollah Muhammed Baqir al-Sadr**, the leading Shi'ite activist killed by Saddam's forces in the late 1980.

His powerbase came from his inherited network of supporters from Sadr City and other Shi'ite Iraqi towns. Drawing on his father's **Sadr Foundation**, Muqtada and his followers distributed food and supplies around Baghdad's suburbs in the first weeks of the 2003 invasion and reopened mosques once the fighting had stopped.

In June 2003, the fiercely anti-U.S. Shi'ite cleric established a militia group called the **Mahdi Army** to help bring about the application of Islamic Law in the country. Believed to command 3,000 to 10,000 guerrillas, the Mahdi Army was named for the hidden Imam that **Twelver Shi'ite** believe will appear in messianic form during the last days of the world. Sadr had convinced his supporters that the Americans had come to Iraq to put down the Shi'ite and prevent them from establishing a Shi'ite religious government in Iraq. As an alternative to the U.S.-dominated Iraqi Governing Council and its successor, the Interim Iraqi Government led by Allawi, Sadr proposed establishing a shadow government based on Islamic principles and ruling by Sharia law.

Sadr also set up a weekly newspaper called **al-Hawza** that was shut down by the coalition authorities at the end of March 2004 on charges of lying about U.S. attacks on the Shi'as and inciting anti-U.S. violence. In response, Sadr mobilized his supporters to protest the closure in a number of Iraqi cities. By the beginning of April, peaceful protests turned violent, engaging the coalition forces in gun battles in Najaf, Sadr City and Basra.

A few months later, Sadr again called on his followers to rise up and fight U.S. troops (who had surrounded his home and exchanged fire with members of Sadr's militia). By August 5th, Sadr's Mahdi Army assaulted a Najaf police station triggering intense clashes between Sadr's supporters and U.S. forces among the cities revered sites, primarily the **Imam Ali shrine** and the adjacent cemetery.

The standoff continued until August 25, 2004 when the **Ayatollah Ali**

Sistani negotiated a cease-fire agreement on his return to Iraq after having had surgery in London.

RIVALRIES

Conflicts among the SCIRI, Sadr Bloc, Al Da'wa and the followers of Grand Ayatollah Ali Sistani were historically driven by the struggle for control of key symbolic places – principally, the shrines of Imam Ali in Najaf and that of his son **Husayn** in Kerbala. Control of the Imam Ali shrine has long been a symbol of resistance.

Sadr vs. Khoei

A few days after **Abd al Majid al-Khoei** returned to Iraq from exile in London in April 2003, he visited the Imam Ali shrine in Najaf accompanied by a controversial Baathist cleric who had been the shrine's caretaker under Hussein's regime. The fact that Khoei had come from London with the blessing and support of the Americans was already a point of contention among Sadr's supporters. And his apparent endorsement of a very unpopular loyalist to the Baathist party, which had been responsible for brutally oppressing the Shi'as was especially disturbing to the Shi'as in the city.

After the two emerged from the mosque of Imam Ali, both the caretaker and Khoei were killed, purportedly by Sadr's follower and possibly on Sadr's orders (Sadr denies the allegation). In 2004 a criminal warrant was issued by the Coalition Provisional Authority and an Iraqi judge for Sadr's arrest in connection with the killing of Khoei in 2003.

Sadr vs. Ayatollah Mohammed Baqir al-Hakim

The Sadr family and the Hakim family both vied over control over the Iraqi Shi'ite community. In September 2003, the Ayatollah was killed in a massive bomb attack. Although it was never confirmed, Sadr was suspected in his death.

Sadr vs. Sistani

The murder of Khoei, the son of Sistani's mentor, fueled the animosity that had been simmering between the moderate cleric, Sistani, and his radical rival, Muqtada Sadr. Politically, Sistani believed that Shi'a clerics should limit their guidance to religious issues and stay out of politics. Conversely, Sadr called for the establishment of a shadow government and popular resistance to the occupation. As Grand Ayatollah, furthermore, Sistani managed millions of dollars in donations from pilgrims and wealthy donors which Sadr coveted. Sadr also raised objections about Sistani's "foreign origin" implying that Sistani's connection with Iran made him unfit to rule in Iraq.

On some occasions, the rivalry over control of holy sites resulted in armed clashes between Al-Sadr's al-Mahdi Army and Sistani's Badr Army.

SUNNI INSURGENCY

The fall of Saddam Hussein brought about the end of a brutal dictatorship. But his demise also resulted in an end to the 80-year old domination of the Iraqi state by the Sunni Arab minority.

SUNNI DOMINANCE

The hegemony of the minority Sunnis began even before the creation of Iraq during the Ottoman Empire when Sunnis were prominent in the administration of the provinces of Baghdad, Basra and, to an extent, Mosul. When the British took over after World War I, they understood the importance of Sunni dominance as a counter to the Shi'a Islamic state of Persia (renamed Iran in 1935). With the installation of Sunni monarch King Faisal on the Iraqi throne, Sunni authority was sealed until the fall of Saddam Hussein's regime in 2003 and the U.S.-coalition drive to establish democratic rule.

The new Coalition Provisional Authority allotted most of its 25 administrative seats to the numerically greater Shi'a Arabs (13 seats) while the non-Kurdish Sunnis received only six seats (Kurds were allotted 4 seats, Assyrians and Turkmen had one seat each).

UNEMPLOYMENT

In the course of the coalition government's de-Baathification drive, moreover, great numbers of Sunni's associated with Saddam's regime were removed from power along with about 450,000 soldiers who had demobilized without pay or pension (but with their weapons) when the Americans decided to disband Iraq's forces. The military had been a refuge for poor youth in the first half of the 20th century and its fighters have been on almost continuous active duty since Iraq's war with Iran beginning in 1980. It's estimated that more than 2 million people had been dependent on pay received from the military.

Other victims of the defeat of the Baathist regime were tribal leaders who had received favors from Saddam in an attempt to extend his influence to the villages. Tribal practices and loyalties dominated in the area of the Sunni Triangle (see box) where concepts of pride and revenge fueled Sunni insurgency – especially among Iraqis who had lost friends or family members in the fighting — against the western occupiers.

The West had long been held accountable for the despair and poverty that resulted from 12 years of sanctions. After the war, the British and Americans were also blamed for the interruption of basic public services (electricity, water and sewage), critical unemployment and lawlessness that beleaguered the country immediately after fighting had ended.

The Iraqis feared that coalition forces had entered the country in order to pillage Iraq's resources, provoking insurgents to sabotage the oil industry by bombing pipelines and other facilities and to impose Western political and economic structures.

Most troubling to Islamists within Iraq and neighboring countries, was the perception that the Christian invaders were intent on abolishing Islam.

Following the trend in the rest of the Muslim world, the Islamic movement in Iraq flourished after decades of repression under the Saddam Hussein's secular regime.

SALAFIS

Most Sunni Iraqis in the **Sunni Triangle** follow the austere "Salafi" or "Wahhabi"[9] branch of Islam practiced in Saudi Arabia.[10] Salafis insist on a literal interpretation of the Quran (Islam's holy book) and advocate returning to the pure Islam of the time of the Prophet Mohammed. They are particularly opposed to foreign and non-Muslim influences on the religion and many see their battle against the "Christian" troops of the coalition forces as a "holy war."

SUNNI TRIANGLE
Area stretching west from Baghdad to the town of Ramadi and north to Tikrit, including Fallujah
AL-ANBAR PROVINCE
A vast area extending from the Syrian border to the western outskirts of Baghdad.

For the Sunni Muslim clerics of **Fallujah** (also called the "City of Mosques" because its estimated 300,000 residents are known for their piety) the invasion presented the opportunity to impose Islamic Sharia law – especially after U.S. Marines gave up control of the city to a local militia (see box below).

The Iraqi cause attracted *mujahideen* (Islamic holy warriors) from Syria, Jordan, Saudi Arabia, Egypt, Sudan and Chechnya who took up the insurgency with violent results.

Among the most dangerous and capable player in this group of foreign fighters was **Abu Musab al-Zarqawi**, a Jordanian-born militant with ties to Al-Qaeda. Zarqawi was believed to be the head of an insurgency group called **Al Tawhid Awl-Jihad** ("Monotheism and Holy Struggle") which was responsible for kidnapping and beheading foreigners, among other atrocities.

METHODS

In order to weaken the hold of the occupiers, Sunni insurgents did whatever they could to sabotage reconstruction efforts by destroying electrical power stations, blowing up oil pipelines, terrorizing foreign contractors and other atrocities. Iraqis accused of collaborating with the western-led governments were assassinated (especially officers in the new Iraqi police force and offi-

---

[9] The name "Wahhabi" is considered derogatory by the Salafists ("early Muslims") since it implies that they revere the founder of the branch, Muhammed bin Abd al-Wahhab. For more on the Salafis, please refer to Roraback, Islam in a Nutshell, Enisen Publishing, 2004.

[10] The CIA has alleged that Saudi Arabia is a leading financier of the Sunni insurgency.

cials and employees of the coalition-led governments) and non-military foreigners were kidnapped and, in some cases, beheaded because their governments failed to give in to stated demands -- usually to withdraw troops from Iraq. Other hostages were held in demand for the release of female Iraqi prisoners from U.S. jails and repeal of French laws prohibiting Muslim schoolgirls from wearing headscarfs among other things.

FALLUJAH (Fallouja, Falluja)

30-40 miles west of Baghdad, Fallujah has been a hotbed of Sunni-led resistance against coalition forces. The city's residents were known for their religious piety: women, in the rare occasions that they were seen in public, covered themselves from head to toe, liquor stores were banned and men donned beards in observance of Islamic tradition.

In April, 2004, coalition forces led a counteroffensive in Fallujah in response to the murder and mutilation of four American contractors. After a three-week siege, the U.S. handed over authority to a local militia called the **Fallujah Brigade** commanded by a former Saddam-era general.

The handover was billed as a victory against the superpower within the city and the ineffectual Fallujah Brigade (now disbanded) couldn't prevent the reassertion of power by hard-line Islamic leaders.

Strict Sharia law was imposed on the residents upon the departure of the US troops and a local Islamic court was installed to dispense Islamic punishments for local crimes (hands were cut off for theft, 80 lashes were given for selling alcohol etc.).

The city became a staging ground for indigenous insurgents and foreign extremists (including many Al-Qaeda operatives) engaged in the "holy war" against the infidel west.

FOREIGN RELATIONS

TURKEY

Economically, Turkey has relied on Iraqi trade, both legal and illegal. Turkey made considerable money from Iraq's oil exports though a pipeline from Iraq to the Turkish port of Ceyhan and even more from smuggling in and out of Iraq, which it justified as compensation for the trade losses resulting from UN sanctions imposed on Iraq.

Turkey was especially concerned with the activities of the Iraqi Kurds, who had enjoyed a considerable amount of self-rule under the protection of the no-fly zone which weakened Hussein's influence in the area. A strong Iraqi Kurdish community, Turks feared, could join with, or provoke their 12-million strong Turkish Kurdish counterparts (the PKK/Kadek) inciting a civil war.

In order to contain Iraq's northern Kurdish population (and guarding their underlying interest in Kirkuk and its oil-fields) the Turks maintained a strong military presence on its border with northern Iraq.

The looming war between the coalition U.K./U.S. forces and Saddam Hussein's regime in 2003 presented an opportunity and a threat for Turkey. With Hussein out of the picture, the Turks could occupy the northern part of the country, subdue the Iraqi Kurds, and take control of the oil-rich Kikuk region. At the same time, the war could strengthen the position and authority of the Iraqi Kurds, helping them realize their ambitions of creating a sovereign state of Kurdistan.

As the only Muslim member of the North Atlantic Treaty Organization (NATO) and a neighbor of Iraq, Turkey played a vital role for the Americans who hoped to use the country as a staging ground for a northern entry into Iraq in March, 2003. In return for stationing 62,000 troops in Turkey in preparation for the war, the US offered the government $15 billion in much needed compensatory aid. The request was denied, though, by Turkey's parliament, which was dominated by the AKP (Islamist Justice and Development Party), reflecting the anti-war sentiments of the Turkish population.As a compromise, Turkey later allowed allied troops to fly over the country.

Turkey tried to deploy security troops to Iraq after the war in order to leverage its position in the political future of a post-Saddam era, curb the military and political position of the Iraqi Kurds and buttress the weakening position of their linguistic and cultural brothers, the Turkomans. The move was violently opposed by the Iraqi Kurdish parties, KDP and PUK.

FRANCE

France and Iraq have been trading partners since 1975 when France's Prime Minister **Jacques Chirac** became the first French leader to meet with Saddam Hussein (then Iraq's vice president and strongman). The next year, Saddam returned the gesture by visiting Chirac in France — his first and only visit to a Western country. According to Chirac, the two became personal friends.

In the course of the meetings, Saddam granted French oil companies a number of privileges and a 23% share in Iraqi oil. In exchange, France sold Iraq an estimated $20 billion worth of weapons including Mirage fighters and Exocet AM39 air-to-surface missiles, and facilitated the construction of Iraq's first nuclear-powered center in Tammuz (the **Osirak** reactor destroyed by Israel in 1980). Until 1991, when relations temporarily chilled after Hussein invaded Kuwait, France was Iraq's second biggest trading partner after Russia in a wide range of civilian goods and services.

After the 1991 Gulf War, France loaned Iraq billions of dollars to help the country rebuild its infrastructure – a debt that remained unpaid because economic sanctions had kept Iraq financially weak. Had the United Nations lifted the embargo, France and Russia would have profited not only from repayment of debts but also from billions of dollars worth of contracts relating to Iraq's oil industry. If Hussein's government was overthrown by the U.S. and Britain, on the other hand, France would lose the money it had invested as well as its privileged trading status in the region.

For that reason, France took great measures to forestall such a conflict by trying to persuade Saddam to step aside in favor of his son, Qusay, by urging UN members to continue their weapons inspection program and, finally, by using the country's United Nations veto power to kill the U.S./U.K. – proposed UN resolution supporting war (see box <u>UN Vote for War</u>, p.25 and The <u>Road to War</u> p.56).

France's fears were realized soon after fighting ended when the U.S. administration barred non-coalition members from bidding on the first round of prime reconstruction contracts. The United States also campaigned for indebted countries to reschedule payments on loans and contracts owed to them by Iraq in order to apply profits from oil sales to reconstruction costs -- thereby lightening America's financial burden (see box <u>Iraq's Debts</u> p. 27).

In 2004, France finally agreed to help train Iraqi security forces and supported limited forgiveness of Iraqi debt since Iraq's financial success was as vitally important to the French as it was to coalition governments. If the U.S. accepted France's help, it was reasoned, they would have to give the French a say over policy.

THE POLITICS OF OIL

Since the turn of the century, when then-British Secretary of State for War and Air **Winston Churchill** decided to convert the Royal Navy from a coal-burning to an oil-burning fleet to gain advantage over the Germans, Middle Eastern oil has played a powerful role in world politics.

Britain, which had no oil of its own, was forced to get the commodity abroad and, like the French, Germans, Russians and Americans, set its sights on the oil potential in the Middle East.

Initially, Britain tapped into newly-discovered oil in Persia by forming the **Anglo-Persian Oil Company** (which became **British Petroleum**). When an entrepreneurial Armenian, **Calouste Gulbenkian**, calculated that oil must also exist underneath the deserts of Mesopotamia, Britain jumped at the opportunity and united with Germany and the **Royal Dutch-Shell Company** to create the **Turkish Petroleum Company** (TPC) in 1912.

The drive for oil intensified a few years later when nations fighting in **World War I** (1914-1918) recognized the importance of oil for military purposes (to fuel naval ships, tanks, trucks, submarines and even military airplanes), and then faced a post-war petroleum shortage.

By 1918, Britain had staked its claim on the potentially oil-rich Ottoman *vilayets* of Baghdad and Basra and was working to secure administrative control over Mosul (which had been promised to France under the secret **Sykes-Picot** agreement that carved-up the Ottoman Empire). The French, who lacked oil themselves, were offered Germany's quarter share in TPC as consolation, along with French dominance over Lebanon and Syria.

But the Anglo-French agreement enraged the Americans, who insisted that they, too, be given a share in the **Oil Company.** To accommodate the U.S., a year after oil was discovered in Kirkuk in northern Iraq (1927), American companies **Jersey Standard** and **Socony** (**Exxon** and **Mobil**) were allotted a 23.75% stake in TPC.

But while the British, French, U.S. and even Gulbenkian (who received a 5% share in TPC and became one of the richest men in the world) all profited from Mesopotamian oil, the Iraqis received nothing until they took matters into their own hands.

IRAQ TAKES CONTROL OVER ITS OIL RESERVES

In 1958, all the members of the British-backed Royal Hashemite family were brutally killed in a military coup led by **General Karim Kassim.** Iraq's new government immediately demanded vast revisions in the concessions of the TPC (now called the **Iraq Petroleum Company** [IPC]) and in the early 1960s revoked 99.5% of IPC's concessions.

Later in the year, Iraq helped create the **Organization of Petroleum Exporting Countries (OPEC)** to help its five founding members (Iraq, Iran, Kuwait, Saudi Arabia and Venezuela) — the source of over 80% of the world's crude oil exports — exercise complete sovereignty over oil production. Although initially OPEC did little for its member countries, the organization later fulfilled its objective by coordinating and unifying petroleum policies in order to establish fair and stable prices for petroleum producers.

After **Kassim's** murder in 1963, the incoming **Baath Party** established the **Iraqi National Oil Company** (INOC) to exploit the areas that had been expropriated from IPC's European members a couple of years earlier.

After the 1967 Arab-Israeli war, which resulted in strong anti-American and anti-British sentiments throughout the Arab world, Iraq began to turn to other countries to help them develop their oil industry, in particular, France and the Soviet Union. Money borrowed from these countries to pay for the exploration and development of their oil fields was to be repaid in crude oil when the oil wells were functional (see Foreign Relations, p. 52)

In 1972, the Baath Party under **Bakr** repealed the remaining .5% of IPC concessions giving Iraq 100% control over its own oil industry. The Iraqi regime used the new oil revenues to fund domestic infrastructure projects, develop transportation projects and make other improvements in the country. Saddam Hussein, who played a prominent role in Bakr's government, saw his own popularity rise as Iraq prospered, facilitating his ascension to the presidency in 1979.

OIL AND THE IRAN-IRAQ WAR
With Iraq's wealth tied to its oil trade, it was imperative to secure the nation's main export routes, including the **Shatt-al-Arab** waterway (Iraq's only access to the Persian Gulf). But the war that Hussein initiated against Iran to secure control over the waterway also interrupted the flow and transport of the nation's most valuable resource.

After eight years of war, Iraq's oil industry was in shambles -- oil wells had been neglected or destroyed in war, the rest of the world had turned to other countries for their petroleum supplies and Iraq's economy was too weak to rebuild the industry. To make matters worse, the world price of oil had dropped precipitously by the late 1980s making economic recovery even more difficult.

OIL AND THE GULF WAR
Saddam blamed Kuwait for most of the country's ills. He accused the Kuwaitis of stealing from the **Rumaila oil field** (which was shared by the two countries) and flooding the oil market thereby driving down prices. In

retaliation, he declared war against the small nation in 1990.

Rather than easing Iraq's economic crisis, though, the war against Kuwait only made matters worse. Sanctions imposed by the UN at the onset of the war blocked the country's oil-trade and the terms of subsequent UN Resolutions put Iraq's oil industry virtually back into foreign hands (in particular **UN Resolution 706** of August, 1991 which stipulated that all profits from petroleum sales from Iraq would be put into an escrow account to be administered by the Security-General of the UN). Without money to maintain oil wells or explore new sources, moreover, Iraq's production levels continued to drop much lower than the country's potential.

Hoping to sway UN voting nations into campaigning for the lifting of economic sanctions, Hussein attempted to woo countries like France, Russia and China by promising them lucrative oil deals if and when sanctions were dropped.

With a greatly diminished petroleum output and stiffly regulated export restrictions, Iraq had been eliminated as a source of competition by other oil producing nations. Consequently, Saudi Arabia, the world's largest producer of oil in the world, (Iraq is the second) became such a dominant oil exporter that nations feared it held an inordinate amount of leverage over world oil prices and supplies. Any move to withhold oil sales by Saudi Arabia for political or ideological reasons could result in economic havoc. Opening up Iraq's oil trade, on the other hand, would again balance the playing field.

Moreover, Iraq's high-quality oil is the cheapest to produce and experts believe that the country has been sitting on billions of barrels worth of untapped oil reserves. As long as Hussein was in power and the sanctions were continued, that potential would remain untapped.

Although U.S. President **George W. Bush** and his administration insisted that oil was not a factor in his decision to go to war with Iraq, the issue remained at the forefront of international debate.

The United States and Britain (the biggest proponents of war against Iraq), would profit greatly if Hussein was unseated from power giving them access to oil fields that were earlier restricted. At the same time, France, Russia and China would lose contracts that had been signed with the Iraqi dictator years ago to develop new oil fields and rehabilitate existing ones once UN sanctions were lifted.

WEAPONS OF MASS DESTRUCTION (WMDs)

Just as vast oil reserves made Iraq economically powerful, the possession of weapons of mass destruction, the regime reasoned, would make Iraq militarily and strategically powerful in the Middle East, especially as a defense against potentially belligerent neighbors such as Iran, Turkey and Israel (which has its own nuclear weapons).

But as a participant in the **Nuclear Non-Proliferation Treaty** and under the provisions of a series of UN Security Council Resolutions, Iraq was legally prohibited from producing and maintaining any weapons of mass destruction. The use of chemical warfare, moreover, had been strictly outlawed since the **Geneva Protocol** was ratified in 1925.

Iraq's blatant disregard for the international prohibitions gave the country a reputation for being a dangerous rogue nation.

NUCLEAR WEAPONS
Iraq began its civilian nuclear program (developing nuclear energy for non-military use) in 1956 when it acquired readily-available documents from the U.S. patent office outlining details of the **Manhattan Project** (the West's first atomic weapons project). In 1962, the plans were used to begin construction on Iraq's first nuclear research reactor.

In 1968, Iraq signed the **Nuclear Non-Proliferation Treaty (NPT)** -- a treaty that obliges its members to forgo the manufacture of nuclear weapons and submit its nuclear materials and facilities to regular inspections by the **International Atomic Energy Agency (IAEA)**. In return for cooperation, NPT member countries get access to nuclear technology and are entitled to have an active reactor as long as it is used for peaceful purposes. Iraq, an oil-rich nation with no apparent need for an alternative energy source, took advantage of its membership in the NPT to cultivate its own nuclear weapons program.

By infiltrating the **IAEA** (Iraqi scientists were installed in the organization to learn its methods and promote Iraq's interests), the Iraqi regime was able to hide its weapons program from the NPT and the world. Meanwhile, teams of scientists (including **Khidir Hamza,** Saddam's self-proclaimed "bombmaker" who exposed details about Iraq's nuclear program after defecting to the U.S. in 1994) scoured foreign countries for parts and materials for its ostensibly "peaceful" nuclear agenda.

Under the noses of the inspectors, Iraq initiated the country's first illicit uranium enrichment project and, in 1974, the country legally pruchased a research reactor from France (named **Osirak** by the French and redubbed **Tammuz I** by Iraq). Despite Hussein's confession in an Arabic-language news magazine that Iraq wanted to be the first Arab nation to engage in nuclear arming, the only foreign country that was alarmed enough to take measures (having used French reactors to built its own nuclear arsenal) was Israel.

In June 1981, Israeli pilots dropped 13 bombs on the new French reactor core, demolishing Osirak (Tammuz) and setting back Iraq's nuclear program by years. Some experts believe that had the Israelis not tageteted Tammuz, Hussein might have had functional nuclear weapons by the time he invaded Kuwait in 1990.

After secretly pursuing a multi-billion dollar nuclear weapons program, Iraq's nuclear potential was curtailed again after the country's defeat in the 1991 Persian Gulf War. In compliance with the cease-fire agreement (as outlined in **UN Security Resolution 687**), the United Nations created a **Special Commission** (UNSCOM) to inspect Iraq's weapons facilities and monitor the country's disarmament.

By the time UN inspectors began their work in Iraq in the 1990s, the regime had already mastered the art of deception -- having hidden prohibited weapons production from the IAEA for years. From the UN Commission's creation in 1991 until inspectors were deported from Iraq in 1998, Hussein and his regime played a cat-and-mouse game with **UNSCOM** by blocking entrances to various facilities, claiming to have destroyed some weapons and denying the production of others.

Despite repeated attempts to sabotage UNSCOM's investigation, though, UN workers quickly discovered and monitored the destruction of stockpiles of chemical and biological weapons and dismantled facilities built to produce them. Inspectors also discovered that Iraq had been producing enriched fuel for atomic wepons and, by studying thousands of confiscated dcocuments, learned how far along Iraq's weapons development program actual was.

The greatest disclosure, though, was made by Saddam's son-in-law **General Hussein Kamel al-Majid,** who had been in charge of Iraq's weapons programs. Fearing the ruthless temper of Saddam's son, **Uday,** Kamel al-Majid and his brother defected to Jordan in 1995 where they revealed intimate details about Iraq's weapons program. Consequently, the Iraqi regime was forced to admit it still possessed a cache of weapons of mass destruction that had been overlooked by the inspectors. The brothers were executed for treason by Hussein's henchmen after they returned to Iraq.

By 1998, Hussein, recognizing that compliance with the inspections would not guarantee the lifting of sanctions, decided to put an end to UN activity. Claiming that American inspectors were spies for the CIA, Hussein first announced that the U.S. would no longer be allowed to participate in UNSCOM activities. Then, on August 5, 1998, he unilaterally cut off inspections altogether.

U.S. President **Bill Clinton,** (who was in the middle of impeachment hearings) threatened to bomb Iraq if Hussein didn't readmit inspectors immediately. Brief miltiary action in December 1998 (**Operation Desert Fox**) was followed by an offer to the Iraqi president -- if Hussein fully complied with renewed inspections for nine months (UNSCOM was to be replaced by the **UN Monitoring, Verification and Inspection Commission [UNMOVIC]**), economic sanctions would be lifted. Hussein refused the deal claiming that Iraq was hiding nothing. Intelligence reports, however, demonstrated that Hussein had continued to assemble an arsenal of weapons of mass destruction while the inspectors were gone. British intelligence reports claiming that Iraq had tried to smuggle significant supplies of uranium from Nigeria, Africa were questioned by nuclear inspectors.

CHEMICAL AND BIOLOGICAL WEAPONS

Unlike nuclear weapons, which can cost millions of dollars and require speicized technological expertise, chemical and biological weapons are easy to make, easy to transport, easy to use and easy to hide. A chemical or biological attack, furthermore, can cause as much damage as a nuclear bomb-- killing thousands of people with a single assault.

Iraq began to research these types of weapons in the 1970s. By the time war broke out against Iran in the 1980s, Hussein's regime was able to produce a number of chemical agents including **mustard gas, CS tear gas** and **tabun.**

At the outset of the war, Iraq used riot control agents in order to secure a fast and easy victory. As the war turned in Iran's favor, though, Hussein began ordering the use of chemical weapons against Iranian troops in hopes of reversing Iraqi territorial losses. In mid-1983, Iraqi troops began to use mustard gas and in 1984, Iraq was the first country to use a nerve agent on the battlefield when it deployed tabun-filled aerial bombs on enemy troops. By 1986, it was estimated that Iraqi chemical warfare was responsible for more than 10,000 casualties. The most lethal doses of chemical and nerve agents, though, were reserved for the Kurds in the north.

Kurdish rebellion were especially problematic in the 1980s while Iraq was engaged in military action against Iran. Iraqi troops stationed in the northern part of the country were being killed by Kurdish rebels as they left their camps for food and water, and some Kurds openly aided Iran. In retaliation, Hussein designed a gruesome punishment for the insurgents.

Testing the effects of various chemical and biological agents, Hussein's infamous cousin **Ali Hassan al-Majid** (aka "**Chemical Ali**") first dumped typhoid spores into Kurdish water supplies in 1987, killing hundreds of people. Later, he used gas attacks to take the lives of another hundred Kurdish villagers. But the most disturbing attack took place in March 1988 against the Kurds living in the border town of **Halabja.**

Canisters filled with the nerve gases tabun, sarin and soman as well as mustard gas were strategically dropped around the village, causing thousands of

Kurdish men, women and children to die almost instantly. The rebellions stopped immediately.

Emboldened by his success, Hussein unleashed another round of chemical attacks on Iranian forces. After eight years of war, the Ayatollah Khomeini was finally compelled to sue for peace.

During the Gulf War, Hussein had ordered his military to fire chemical weapons on coalition troops if they reached Baghdad. But when the coalition stopped short of the capital (and in light of U.S. threats of retaliation with nuclear weapons), fire was held. Although there is still no evidence that unconventional weapons were used against coalition forces in the 1990s, reports from Gulf War soldiers complaining of respiratory problems, fatigue, skin rashes, headaches, intestinal problems and other ailments (collectively called "**Gulf War Syndrome**") have led to suspicions that some foul play had occurred.

After years of post-war inspections (per Resolution 687) and the consequent destruction of stockpiles of chemical weapons and the facilities that produce them, the West believed that Hussein still had the abilty to reestablish its chemical warfare program at any time. Experts said it was possible that Iraq concealed several dozen warheads that could be filled with chemical or biological weeapons and launched at Israel, Saudi Arabia or other neighboring nations. It was also believed that the country had caches of deadly chemicals at its disposal. Production of chemical and biological agents could easily be undertaken in "dual-use" facilties (buildings for industrial and commercial use that could be quickly converted for miltiary use), or even portable laboratories, without detection.

THE ROAD TO WAR – UN RESOLUTIONS

660 (Adopted August 2, 1990)
Condemns the Iraqi invasion of Kuwait. Demands that Iraq withdraw immediately and unconditionally all of its forces back to the position held on August 1, 1990.

661 (August 6, 1990)
Determines that Iraq has failed to comply with Resolution 660. Decides that no countries shall import any commodities or products originating in Iraq or Kuwait.

687 (April 3, 1991)
Declares a formal cease-fire between Iraq, Kuwait and the coalition forces. Demands the restoration of friendly relations between Iraq and Kuwait.

Decides that Iraq shall destroy or remove all chemical and biological weapons and all related components and research related to the development of such weapons as well as ballistic missiles with a range greater than 150 kilometers (shorter than the distance to Israel).

Decides that Iraq shall submit a declaration of the locations, amounts and types of items specified above and agrees to on-site inspections.

Decides that a Special Commission will be formed to carry out immediate on-site inspection of Iraq's biological, chemical and missile capabilities, based on Iraq's declarations.

Decides that Iraq shall unconditionally agree not to acquire or develop nuclear weapons or nuclear-weapons-usable material or any sub systems or components or any research, development, support or manufacturing facilties related to the above.

Decides that Iraq shall return all Kuwaiti property seized by Iraq, including a list of any property that Kuwait claims has not been returned or which has not been returned intact.

Decides that all Iraqi statements repudiating its foreign debt are null and void and demands that Iraq adhere scrupulously to all its obligations concerning servicing and repayment of its foreign debt.

Decides that the embargo shall not apply to foodstuffs nor to materials and supplies essential to civilian needs.

Decides that the economic embargo will be lifted if Iraq complies with the resolutions outlined above.

Requires Iraq to declare that it will not commit or support any act of international terrorism or allow any organization directed towards com mission of such acts to operate within its territory.

688 (April 5, 1991)
Condemns the repression of the Iraqi civilian population in many parts of Iraq, including in Kurdish populated areas.

699 (June 17, 1991)
Confirms that the Special Commission and the IAEA have the authority to conduct activities under resolution 687 (1991), for the purpose of supervising the destruction, removal or rendering harmless of the items specified in that resolution.

706 (August 15, 1991)
(Oil-for-food) Permits all countries to import petroleum and petroleum products from Iraq. Decides that payment for petroleum products will be put into an escrow account to be administered by the Secretary-General of the UN and used for the purchase of foodstuffs, medicines and materials and supplies for essential civilian needs and to pay for costs incurred by the UN in facilitating the return of all Kuwaiti property seized by Iraq.

986 (April 14, 1995)
Expands the "oil-for-food" exceptions to the trade embargo and authorizes Turkey to import petroleum and petroleum products from Iraq through the Kirkuk-Yumurtalik pipeline as long as it does not exceed prescribed limits and complies with terms outlined in resolution 706.

1060 (June 12, 1996)
Deplores the refusal of the Iraqi authorities to allow access to sites by UNSCOP in a clear violation of the provisions of Security Council resolution 687.

1134 (October 23, 1997)
Condemns the repeated refusal of the Iraqi authorities to allow access to certain sites by UNSCOM in violation of resolution 687.

1137 (November 12, 1997)
Condemns Iraqi restrictions on access by UNSCOM.

1194 (September 9, 1998)
Condemns Iraq's lack of cooperation with the Special Commission and IAEA.

1205 (November 5, 1998)
Condemns the decision made by Iraq on October 31, 1998 to cease cooperation with the Special Commission as a flagrant violation of resolution 687 (1991) and other relevant resolutions.

1284 (December 17, 1999)
Establishes, as a subsidiary body of the Council, the United Nations Monitoring, Verification and Inspection Commission (UNMOVIC) – to replace UNSCOM.

1441 (November 8, 2002)
Declares Iraq in material breach of its obligations under past resolutions (in particular 687) through Iraq's failure to cooperate with UN inspectors and

the IAEA.

Decides to offer Iraq a final opportunity to comply with disarmament obligations. Iraq shall provide to UNMOVIC and IAEA and Council no later than 30 days from date of the resolution complete declaration of all aspects of its programs to develop chemical, biological and nuclear weapons, ballistic missiles and other delivery systems.

The resolution also "recalls that Iraq has been warned that it will face serious consequences if it continues to violate its obligations."

SPAIN, UK, NORTHERN IRELAND AND US PROVISIONAL RESOLUTION (March 7, 2003)

Not passed (see <u>Votes for War Resolution</u>, p. 25)

Reaffirms the need for full implementation of resolution 1441. Decides that Iraq will have failed to take the final opportunity afforded by resolution 1441 unless on, or before March 17, 2003, the Council concludes that Iraq has demonstrated full, unconditional, immediate and active cooperation in accordance with its disarmament obligations under Resolution 1441 and is yielding to UNMOVIC and IAEA of all weapons, weapon delivery and support systems and structures prohibited by resolution 687.

POST-WAR RESOLUTIONS

1483 (May 22, 2003)

Declares an end of sanctions, in force since 1990, and recognizes Britain and the US as occupying powers ("The Authority") and calls on them to improve security and stability.

1551 (October 16, 2003)

Recognizes the legitimacy of the temporary Coalition Provisional Authority, welcomes the Governing Council as an interim administration and urges them to move towards self-government under UN auspices.

Calls on the UN to strengthen its role in Iraq, authorises a multinational security force and urges states to contribute to the reconstruction of Iraq.

****

Other books by Amanda Roraback:
AFGHANISTAN in a Nutshell, ISLAM in a Nutshell, PAKISTAN in a Nutshell, ISRAEL-PALESTINE in a Nutshell

Please also look for future Nutshell Notes:
on *Iran, Korea, Indonesia, China, Russia, Mexico, Sudan* etc.

For more information about Enisen Publishing and for additional and updated information about Iraq, please visit www.enisen.com.